THE LIFE
JOHN MURRAY

THE LIFE OF
JOHN MURRAY

Iain H. Murray

THE BANNER OF TRUTH TRUST

THE BANNER OF TRUTH TRUST
3 Murrayfield Road, Edinburgh EH12 6EL, UK
P.O. Box 621, Carlisle, PA 17013, USA

*

© The Banner of Truth Trust, 2007

First published in *The Collected Writings
of John Murray*, Volume 3, 1982

First paperback edition, 1984
This reset edition with a
new appendix, 2007

*

ISBN-10: 0 85151 950 4
ISBN-13: 978 0 85151 950 0

*

Typeset in 11/15 pt Adobe Caslon at
the Banner of Truth Trust, Edinburgh
Printed in the U.S.A. by
Versa Press, Inc.,
East Peoria, IL

Contents

Preface

JOHN MURRAY AND I did not belong to the same family, and therefore when, in 1973, we were discussing the publication of his *Collected Writings*, to my proposal that it should include a biography he replied: 'Regarding biographical data, I think I should have to supply a good deal of the information . . . If I supplied a skeleton, perhaps you yourself could write the biographical account.' Thereafter he and I continued our usual correspondence respecting the publishing work of the Banner of Truth Trust, in which he was so influential as a Trustee, but we did not carry that particular proposal any further. The first volume of his *Collected Writings* was not ready for printing; I entertained no doubt about his continuing fitness, and consequently I felt no urge to proceed with speed.

Sadly, therefore, nothing in these pages was provided by our late friend whose health deteriorated so rapidly before his death on 8 May 1975. In the summer of that same year I put together 'A Memorial with Tributes' in a double-issue of *The Banner of Truth* magazine. This present biography is an enlargement of that material, containing additional information at many points. To those who remember John as a friend and a servant of Christ it will be a very inadequate account. Six years after his death there are many across the world who do not cease to miss him deeply. But my hope is that for those who did not know him, and who will thank God for his writings in days yet to come, these pages will provide at least some idea of what he was.

I am indebted to numerous friends for aid without which this biography could not have been written. They include Paul Woolley, David and Calvin Freeman, John Mitchell, Robert S. Sinclair, Grace Mullen, Geoffrey Thomas, Elizabeth Tallach, Allan Harman, Walter J. Chantry, Norman Shepherd, Allan MacRae, S. M. Houghton, Cornelius Van Til, and Lawrence R. Eyres. Especial thanks are due to Arthur Kuschke, Jr, and to Mrs Valerie Murray herself.

IAIN H. MURRAY
Edinburgh,
24 September 1981

Publisher's Note

Since *The Life of John Murray* was originally published, further correspondence of Professor Murray has come to light, particularly the set of letters to Mr Jack Green of Pontefract, Yorkshire, now included as an Appendix (pp. 209–20).

Attention is also drawn to the *Collected Writings of John Murray* in four volumes, publication of which was not complete when the *Life* was written. These throw further light on John Murray's work and contribution to Reformed theology (ISBN 0 85151 396 4).

January 2007

1

The Youngest Son of Badbea

I N THE REMOTE PARISH of Creich, Sutherland, in the North-East Highlands of Scotland, Alexander Murray passed away in 1942 at the age of ninety years. Before that day came he had taken care to secure from his minister a solemn promise that no obituary of him would be published in his Church's magazine. 'He would rather get a slap than flattery', men had said of him in his lifetime. His son, in whose memory these pages are now written, breathed the same spirit. He spoke little and seldom of himself. When, some years ago, a leading American publisher asked him to supply information on his life to be included in a major publication to which he was contributing, his response was characteristic:

John Murray: Professor of Systematic Theology
M.A. Glasgow, 1923; Th.B., Th.M. Princeton
Theological Seminary, 1927.

These brief words, together with the titles of his books which he added, were, in his judgment, sufficient. In part, we may attribute this reticence of father and son to the native reserve of the Highland Gael. Surely no race of men ever disapproved more strongly than they of any broadcasting of personal affairs to the world at large! But in this matter it was the gospel itself and not temperament which exerted the greater influence. One of John Murray's earliest sermons, which he had to hand in as class-work for Senior Homiletics during his preparation for the ministry in the 1920s, was on the words of John the Baptist recorded in John 3:29–30: 'He that hath the bride is the bridegroom: but the friend of the bridegroom, which standeth and heareth him, rejoiceth greatly because of the bridegroom's voice: this my joy therefore is fulfilled. He must increase, but I must decrease.' After an introduction, setting the words in their context, the ministerial student divided his text as follows:

'1. John knew Christ's supreme and exclusive position in the kingdom of God.

2. He knew his 'own subordinate place in the kingdom of God.

3. John knew the only method of development, 'He must increase, but I must decrease.'

Upon this last statement in the text he said:

We are not to think of these words as spoken in Stoical, disappointed submission, but as the expression of a heart full of holy joy that the goal on which he had set his heart had now been actually achieved. His popularity, his increase at the expense of the honour of Christ, would have been his deepest sorrow. We may discover in this, pain of indignation and contempt for the very suggestion of his usurping the place that belonged to Christ alone. . . . The desire for self-supremacy is an expression of the sin which above all others seeks to undermine the very purpose of the gospel and the gospel ministry, which is the restoration of the kingdom of God and the rule and supremacy of God alone in all spheres and departments of life. May God grant that we follow in the footsteps of John and imitate his self-effacement, self-abasement, self-renunciation, self-forgetfulness! 'God forbid that I should glory, save in the cross of our Lord Jesus Christ, by whom the world is crucified unto me, and I unto the world.'

It was the strength of this holy ambition that led John Murray, and the community of Christians amongst whom he was first nurtured in Christ, to deplore the thought of making a name for themselves before men. As he was to write in later years, 'Humility, contrition, lowliness of mind are of the essence of godliness.' And again, in lecturing once on John Calvin, he warned his hearers, 'At all times we must remember that men, however great their stature, are still only men characterized by infirmity, earthen vessels into which God has put treasure, and our servants for Jesus' sake.' He would have regarded it as a serious disservice to the cause of the gospel if a record of his life failed to impress the reader with the truth that praise for any talent or grace belongs to God alone.

John Murray was born in his parents' home at Badbea,[1] Migdale, on 14 October 1898. For beauty the location can scarcely be excelled by anything else in Scotland. The house, or croft, with its surrounding farmland, stands just 150 yards above the edge of Migdale Loch, facing southwards and with rising ground giving the homestead shelter from north winds. Migdale, with its few other crofts similar to the Murray home, is surrounded by hills, 500 to 700 feet in height, the arable ground nearest the loch merging soon into moor land with clumps of trees – larch, mountain ash, Scotch fir and birch.

Hidden from view behind the hills on the southern side of Loch Migdale, and two miles distant, are the waters of the Dornoch Firth, but rising above these nearer hills are the distant peaks of the mountains of Easter Ross in majestic panorama. There are thus simultaneously presented to the eye views both near and far, with a richness of colour capable of all manner of variations depending upon the season or the weather. Writing many years after his infancy in Badbea and its environment John Murray was to say:

Scotland is very hilly country. Along the coasts however there is a good deal of flat farmland and it is very fertile. I don't know any

[1] Badbea: Gaelic, 'A clump of birch'.

farmland in the world where agriculture is more intensively and scientifically carried on than within fifteen miles of my home. And, indeed there are some of the finest farms within a radius of eight miles. My home is only two miles from salt water and only twelve miles from the open ocean. We have kitchen, sitting-room, parlour, and a small bedroom downstairs, and three bedrooms and bathroom upstairs. It is a simple country home. The barns are right on the same line as the dwelling house. There are 30 acres arable land and in addition hill pasture for sheep.

Gospel light appears to have been brought to the district after the sixteenth-century Reformation by a certain Donald Logan who was appointed to the parish of Creich as 'a reader in Gaelic' (*i.e.*, a catechist) but it was not until the eighteenth century that the gospel began to take powerful hold upon the scattered population, especially under the ministry of the Rev. George Rainy from 1771 to 1810. When Rainy died more than one hundred men in the parish 'could openly testify to a personal work of grace and give a reason for the hope that was in them'. The strength of this work, and the deep root it took in many households, may be judged by the fact that from 1810 to 1843 the Christians in Creich maintained their assemblies without a minister; for when Murdo Cameron, a Moderate minister, was intruded into the Parish in 1811, the congregation left him largely to himself and for two years, summer and winter, met on the shores of Loch Migdale under the shelter of a great rock near Badbea. Thereafter, for the convenience of the people (in a parish thirty-five miles long) two separate meeting places were appointed. When visiting ministers preached in the parish the congregation would again assemble in the church but they steadfastly refused to hear their own minister. Yet it was clear that Cameron was not wholly unsympathetic, for he would regularly invite to the Summer Communion season (always held in the third week of August) two of the leading evangelical preachers of the Highlands, John MacDonald of Ferintosh and John Kennedy of Redcastle. With the Disruption of the Church of Scotland in 1843, the people at once united with the newly formed Free Church of Scotland and called Gustavus Aird to be their minister. There were 280 signatures to the call.[1]

The health of the work prior to 1843 depended upon four elders who were the sole guides and leaders of the people. To their number eight more were added in 1844. These were men eminent for their spiritual gifts and they spread light and warmth throughout the whole parish. The story is told of how one of them, Havie Munro, as a young man under spiritual concern, found himself walking to a monthly fellowship meeting behind Hugh Mackenzie, an older Christian whose godliness filled him with awe. Not wishing to pass Mackenzie, Munro slackened his pace only to find another such man coming up behind him. 'I felt', he said afterwards, 'as between two fires from heaven'! In old age the same Munro confessed to a friend that sometimes, when favoured with much of the Divine presence, he had erred in praying, *Cum air ais do làmh* ('Stay thine hand'), for he felt he should have prayed for increased strength to 'take in' what was given him. Another of these devout elders, Hugh Mann, who was very deaf in later years, was so eager not to miss the Word that he would mount the pulpit steps and stand close to the minister!

Men of this type long adorned the parish of Creich and Dr Aird 'often confessed to a sense of utter want of fitness to preside over such a session'. It is no small testimony to the high esteem in which the church held John Murray's father that he was ordained to the eldership at the early age of twenty-seven. Alexander

---

[1] This, and other information in this chapter, is taken from Alexander MacRae, *The Life of Gustavus Aird,* Stirling, n.d.

Murray was born in 1853. As an old man he could remember how, when an infant, a relative taught him the prayer as she put him to bed, 'Create in me a clean heart, O God; and renew a right spirit within me.' He recalled, also, as a youth being able to count no less than eight prayer-meetings being held on a Saturday evening in an area of some three square miles around Badbea. After his marriage to Catherine Logan (probably a descendant of Donald Logan) his own home was to become one of the most frequent resorts of Christians meeting for fellowship and prayer. Christ himself was often there, as in Bethany of old, and the hospitality afforded to all who came was known throughout the North.

John was the youngest of the family, being preceded by five brothers and two sisters. In the early 1890s far-reaching changes, some of which were beneficial, had come to the parish. Throughout much of the century the crofters of Sutherland had endured considerable hardship and even deprivation at the hands of the proprietors upon whose land they lived as tenants. The Creich parish fell within Skibo, an estate containing around 20,000 acres, only some 6,000 of which were arable ground. Tenant crofters had often to live as best they could off largely infertile soil and at the same time pay exorbitant rents to grasping proprietors. It was, as Dr Aird protested in 1884, 'a first-class manufactory for producing paupers'. In a statement before a Royal Commission, Aird pointed out that the rents collected from the Skibo estate had risen from £700–800 in 1793 to £4,813 in 1884, compelling the emigration of large numbers from his parish, 'upwards of 266 to Australia and 100 to America, besides a considerable number to the large centres of population in the south'.

In May 1898, however, as Catherine Murray was carrying her sixth son, the prospects brightened. Towards the end of that month Alexander had to go down to Bonar Bridge, the nearest village, two miles distant, to join with other tenants to welcome the new proprietor of Skibo Castle and estate. It was Andrew Carnegie, with his wife Louise, returning to his native country after making a huge fortune from the companies which in the following year he formed into the Carnegie Steel Company of the United States. His tenants, who presented him with an address of welcome, cared nothing for his political faith and his 'gospel of wealth', but his ability to provide work was a much-needed benefaction. At Skibo Castle, where the Stars and Stripes now hung alongside the Union Jack, £50,000 was at once spent on building a new wing, and soon Carnegie wanted old roads remade and new ones built to provide access to lochs and moors for shooting and fishing. In the latter operation 'Sandy' Murray played a considerable part. He became a contractor employed by Carnegie to organize and lead squads of men on the road work and so efficient was he at levelling ground that he was popularly known as 'Sandy Level'! For such work he was well qualified both by physical strength and moral integrity: it was common knowledge that when Sandy Murray received payment for work done he kept not a penny more for himself than he gave to each of his men.

Far off though it was from the great debates and controversies which were then agitating the Free Church in the South, the tremors of those events were being felt with growing dismay in Sutherland before the 1890s. There was growing alienation between the weakening evangelicalism in the South and the old orthodoxy which remained widespread in the North. After heresy charges, well sustained by evidence, were brought against certain Free Church theologians, only to be dismissed, the likelihood of a further disruption grew imminent. When the old worthies of Creich heard Alexander Whyte of Edinburgh preach at a communion season in the parish they did not like certain new notes which they detected. In 1893 a crisis was precipitated by the withdrawal of two Highland ministers, Donald Macfarlane and

Donald Macdonald, who sought to maintain the gospel in its purity by the formation of the Free Presbyterian Church. The godly were divided; some of the best of the people in the North joined the new Church but others, including Dr Aird, remained, judging that no constitutional change had been made in the old Free Church sufficient to justify separation. As for Alexander Murray, in 1895, despite his love for his minister, he decided that he could remain in his session no longer. When, after more than fifty years' ministry, Aird preached his last sermon in Creich in November 1896, Alexander Murray was already worshipping in the newly-formed Free Presbyterian Church. The Creich Free Church, handsomely rebuilt in 1881, was the only manmade landmark of any size visible from Badbea and it was with aching hearts that the Murrays could no longer view it as their spiritual home.

John, the new baby in Badbea, was baptized at the communion season in the spring of 1899 by Neil Cameron, the Free Presbyterian minister of Glasgow.

The accommodation at Badbea was stretched to the limits when the last member of the family was born. The present house, described above, was not built until 1906. Prior to that date, John's Grandmother Murray, with unmarried son and daughter, occupied one-half of the long croft house and Alexander Murray and his family the other half. John remembered his grandmother (who died in 1906) speaking in Gaelic with his mother. 'Johnnie' Murray – also to be known locally as 'Johnnie Level' – and his next older brother, unlike the older children, were brought up to speak English. Until he was six he shared a bed with his two sisters, Johan and Christina, but at that age he determined to sleep henceforth with his older brothers. He was a quiet child, yet not incapable of mischief. On one occasion, when his brothers were going out to burn stubble after the harvest, in order to pacify their infant brother (whom they did not want to take) they gave him a few matches. To do his own 'burning' Johnnie proceeded to make a little pile of oats which, once alight, to his great consternation blew into the stack from which he had taken them. With the whole stack now blazing he was so upset that he retired quietly from the scene and as others raised the alarm he was found sitting alone indoors. His father did not punish him. Rather he explained the seriousness of losing the harvest. But sometimes there were punishments, and John, like most children, soon learned that the telling of a lie was a possible way to escape what he deserved. For a time he was tempted to practise that art, but in later years he remembered how, about the age of seven, in the very midst of a team race at school, he vowed as he ran from one point to another that he would tell lies no more. Another childhood memory was the occasion when, discovered by a teacher in the midst of a fight, he heard the question, 'What if your father saw you like this?'

Not only upon the Sabbath, when the family walked towards Bonar Bridge to join the forty or fifty who met in the Free Presbyterian Church, but every day of the week, John was surrounded by Christian influence. At Badbea the day commenced and closed with prayer and praise. It should be specially mentioned that no portion of Scripture had more pervasive influence upon the family religion of that period than the Psalter. Those inspired songs were found suitable for all circumstances. Dr Aird once told the story how, some years earlier, when eighteen poor families were ruthlessly evicted from their homes by the proprietor of the land, they took what shelter they could in a graveyard and began their family worship together that sad day with the singing of Psalm 145 from verse fifteen:

> The eyes of all things wait on thee,
> The giver of all good;
> And thou, in time convenient,
> Bestow'st on them their food.

Thine hand thou open'st liberally,
And of thy bounty gives
Enough to satisfy the need
Of ev'ry thing that lives.

But if John Murray saw parental godliness in acts of worship he saw it no less in all the daily practical labours in which his father engaged. Piety and hard work went hand in hand. 'The people are very industrious', Aird reported to the Royal Commission in 1884, 'and so far as I remember, I do not know a lazy man in my congregation.' This was sure result of that God-consciousness which lies at the centre of true spirituality. The Christians of Creich, amongst whom the head of Badbea's household was a leader, were as mindful of their relationship to God when farming land or making roads as they were in church. All daily toil must be undertaken for the glory of God. Though their numbers were growing thin in comparison with former times, there were still many men and women in Sutherland at the beginning of the twentieth century who exemplified the Pauline injunction: 'Whatsoever ye do, do it heartily, as to the Lord, and not unto men; knowing that of the Lord ye shall receive the reward of the inheritance: for ye serve the Lord Christ' (*Col.* 3:23–24).

Notwithstanding Alexander Murray's work as a road contractor the members of his large family were compelled to live very simply. For long, at the main meal of the day, all that was on the table was potatoes and herring. 'How poor we were in those days', John reflected in later years.[1] But it was a happy family, and love

---

[1] Poverty was a long struggle for the people of Sutherland. Another John Murray of the mid-nineteenth century, was one day visited by a fellow clansman who, receiving the family's usual mid-day meal of potatoes and salt, expressed his sympathy 'that the potatoes are so poor'. To which John replied, 'There is not one of them on which I do not see the beauty of the Blood.' This same John Murray was once praying for guidance by a riverside at a time when

for every stone of Badbea was their common inheritance. When John was about six years old it was remembered how one day he looked up and said to his grown-up brother Alex: 'If my father dies would *you* be wanting this place?' He replied: 'I don't know, Johnnie: why are you asking?' To which the boy answered: 'Well, if you do not want it, I'd like it myself'!

The Free Presbyterian minister of Bonar Bridge in those days was Ewen MacQueen who, when he visited Badbea, had the habit of putting his hand on John's head and saying a few words to him affectionately about spiritual things. It was not known to Mr MacQueen at the time, but in later years John Murray spoke of those occasions as being accompanied by the first stirrings of spiritual emotion which he could recall. He also remembered Mr MacQueen as an amazing man who wore three overcoats and whose roaring bedroom fire, whenever he stayed with them, required the carrying of several extra loads of peat! In other Free Presbyterian ministers, and particularly in John Cameron of Tomatin and John MacDonald of Gairloch, he also witnessed practical godliness of a high order. When no minister could be present on the Sabbath, his father would preach. These were by no means the only times when the father urged upon his son the glory of the Saviour's grace. John remembered, for example, a day when he travelled with his father over the fifteen miles of the County road between Bonar Bridge and the Mound near Golspie, via Loch Buie, which Alexander Murray was under contract to maintain. Though they covered the considerable distance by horse and

---

many were emigrating to America. While so engaged he heard a thud on the grass beside him as a salmon leaped clean out of the water. This he took as an answer: the Lord could provide for him in Sutherland! Murray, it should be said, is one of the most common names in Sutherland. 'Old Creich Memories', in *The Monthly Record of the Free Church of Scotland*, 1927, p. 108.

cart, Sandy Murray was throughout imparting spiritual counsel to his son. With reference to his father on that occasion John Murray once told his nephew that 'he did not witness a greater intensity of spiritual exercise of soul in any other person and his very body moved in sympathy with the inner man.'

John Murray's school days were passed first at the local Bonar Bridge School, and then at the Dornoch Academy, where brighter pupils went at about the age of twelve to study for the Higher Certificate necessary for university entrance. The Academy, being some fourteen miles from Badbea, was reached after a cycle ride early on Monday mornings, and lodgings in Dornoch were occupied until late Friday afternoon. He proved an excellent scholar and in his eighteenth year the Academy, which found it very difficult to engage suitable staff, used him for a time as a tutor.

Such was the youth's first experience of absence from home. His second was of a far darker nature. The effects of the First World War on the Scottish Highlands were almost as devastating as if it had been fought on that soil. When the conflict began in 1914 the long-famous Highland regiments at once claimed the cream of the manhood of the North; but very few who were recruited at the beginning of the conflict ever returned to their homes. Of John's brothers, William went to the Navy, Donald went to France with the Seaforth Highlanders, and Thomas to the Dardanelles with the Cameron Highlanders An eye-witness on the day when Thomas left Badbea spoke of it as one of the most affectionate partings he ever witnessed between a loving father and a dutiful son. The thick-set and soft-spoken father put his arms around Tommy's neck – the boy who had never said 'No' to him – and Tommy embraced his father: 'Goodbye, Tommy, I'll never see you again' were among his final words before he watched his son ride off on a white horse. And so it was to prove. Thomas was killed in action. John's call-up for military service was dated 18 April 1917, when he was enlisted in the Royal Highlanders (Black Watch) at Nairn. On official papers he is described as Private Murray, 5/22863; 'Height, 5 ft 6½ in; Complexion, Fresh; Eyes, Brown; Hair, Black'. It appears that he did his initial army training at Perth and that later he was sent to a camp at Bridge of Allan. At the latter place his older brother Donald came to visit him one weekend on his way back to France after a short stay in hospital. They talked of spiritual things as they walked together on the banks of the river Allan. It was their last meeting.

Among the few possessions bestowed on John by the army was a pocket-sized paperback, which he was to retain all his days, *The Story of the Black Watch*, being an account of the regiment's 'heroic failures, splendid successes, and undying glories'. In France, however, the Black Watch, along with all the allied infantry, were fighting a campaign which permitted few such exploits as had been performed in earlier days. In the face of shells and machine-guns they were constantly decimated and consequently new recruits were kept at home for no longer than the minimum period necessary for training. It seems likely that John Murray was sent across the English Channel before the end of 1917.

By the time John arrived in France his brother Donald had already been posted as 'missing-in-action', the location of his presumed death being unknown. John's concern and efforts to obtain more definite information and to trace a grave were unavailing. He came to believe that Donald had been wounded and had fallen into a shell hole. Among the comparatively few items which John was to keep among his personal possessions until the end of his days was a map of the sector of France where they had both served.

Appallingly uncongenial as the trenches were for humanity in general, they were yet more distressing to a Christian: the sight of men dosed well with rum in preparation for battle, and the hardened paganism of the ungodly in the presence of death, promoted feelings distressing in the extreme. John Murray was not commonly known to identify his conversion with any single date or experience in his youth; unlike his own father, who was brought suddenly from intense conviction of sin to peace in believing, it is possible that he was only gradually aware of the presence of true spiritual life within.[1] Conversion for some, as he used to say, is like the gentle dawn of day in northern latitudes when there is no exact moment observable which separates the night from the day. What is clear is that during his days in the Black Watch, spiritual realities were his main concern; whenever there was any opportunity for relaxation he would draw aside from his comrades and find some corner where he might read his Bible and pray.

As the Great War came to its climax in 1918, strain and sorrow cast their long shadows in the once-sun-lit rooms of the old home beside Migdale. Long intervals passed between news of victories or reverses at the battle front with confirmation that the youngest son was still alive. As Alexander Murray continued in prayer there was one sentence of Scripture which repeatedly comforted him. He recalled how, when John was baptized in the peaceful spring of 1899, not only were God's covenant promises his confidence, but certain words in Psalm 92 had spoken to him so forcefully that he believed their fulfilment would be seen in the infant carried in his arms: 'Those that be planted in the house of the LORD shall flourish in the courts of our God. They shall still bring forth fruit in old age.' John, he was persuaded, would return from the War.

It appears that when the last German offensive began in July 1918, John was posted as missing; then this was corrected by news that he had been wounded in action and removed from the battle front to hospital. The facts appear to be that day after day, during the last great German drive, John's regiment would stand and

[4] Valerie Murray recalls him expressing the belief that he had known Christ from his childhood.

fight, lose many of its men, and be forced into rapid retreat. When evening came those who survived would be asleep from exhaustion almost before they could lie down on the ground. On one occasion John fell asleep leaning against a piece of farm machinery and still wearing his full pack. After three days of battle, however, all along the front line, the enemy offensive was stopped and the Allied advance, the final turning point in the War, began. In later years John spoke of the new exhilaration at seeing the kilted Scots moving forward, taking position after position. But his participation in the success was short-lived. While leading a section of men, as a lance corporal, and in the act of firing his rifle he was, as he believed, temporarily blinded in his 'shooting eye' by dirt thrown up from a bursting shell. The truth was that the sight of his right eye had been irretrievably destroyed by shrapnel. From a first-aid post, where he stopped to have his eye washed, he was at once ordered back to the rear, then to a base hospital, and before the day was over, he was on a train headed for the Channel. Soon he was in an English hospital where, a few days later, his eye was removed. His convalescent period was spent in London, his first visit to the English capital. On 10 December 1918, he was discharged, 'being no longer physically fit for war service', and in due course received the customary scroll inscribed, 'Served with honour and was disabled in the Great War.' A small pension was subsequently paid.

The glass eye which John Murray wore, so closely resembled the original that even those who knew him well tended to forget that his sight was limited to one eye. It was a considerable handicap for one whose next ten years were to be given to almost unremitting study. He entered the University of Glasgow in the autumn of 1919 and, in the hope that less strain would be placed on his eyesight, his Arts course in Logic, Moral Philosophy, Institutes of Education, Mathematics, Latin, and English Literature, was extended over four years instead of three. The M.A. degree was conferred upon him on 20 June 1923. At one time, it seems, his inclinations were divided: he felt a pull to both Mathematics and Theology and knew that his future career could not contain both. By the time he graduated in 1923 his mind was decisively made up, captured by the conviction that he considered an essential part of the call to the Christian ministry, 'Woe is unto me, if I preach not the gospel!' He was by this time a communicant member of the Free Presbyterian Church and had preached his first sermon in Stratherick, Inverness-shire, in 1922 upon the words, 'His name shall be called Wonderful'. On 16 August 1923, the Kirk Session of the Bonar Bridge congregation examined him as a candidate for the ministry and recommended him to the Northern Presbytery of the Church, which met the following day and approved the recommendation.

Accordingly John Murray commenced the three-year period of theological study required by his Church. Comparatively small in numbers, the denomination did not maintain a college, preferring instead the time-honoured procedure of placing their students for the ministry under the supervision of a minister who would undertake to tutor them while also occupying a pastoral charge. Donald Beaton, minister in Wick, Caithness, had long and ably undertaken this role, and it was therefore to Wick that John Murray went, along with five other theological students, in the autumn of 1923. Robert Sinclair, a fellow student of that period, remembers John as possessing his father's self-composure, as notable for his kindness, and as a student and a preacher of more than common ability. The latter fact soon impressed Mr Beaton, and he formed the conviction that the best interests of the Church would be served if Murray's training could be more advanced in certain departments than was possible in Wick. The result was that the Synod of the Free Presbyterian Church, meeting in May 1924, heard the unusual suggestion from their theological tutor 'that Mr John Murray, M.A., be permitted to proceed to Princeton, with a view of taking up the study of certain subjects to equip him as a theological tutor of the Church'. The Synodical Report records that 'the suggestion was received with the heartiest approval'. So in the summer of 1924, John Murray took his first trans-Atlantic voyage from Glasgow to New York.

His first day on American soil can hardly have been a happy experience. With all other immigrants at that period, sometimes as many as five thousand a day, he had to land on the 27-acre Ellis Island before setting foot in New York. A number was given him before he left the ship; then, jostling with others, with bags and baskets, he had to enter the lower floor of the Great Registry Hall, climb a long staircase and pass a hurried medical check at the top before entering the reception room with its 56-foot high vaulted ceiling. Entrance through Ellis Island was by no means automatic. An average of two out of every hundred people were sent back; others had to wait in dormitories for days or weeks before they were finally cleared. For reasons unknown to us, John Murray was put among those who were thus detained. Perhaps he had not been warned in advance of the twenty-nine questions he had to answer in that reception room. He certainly had no 'work permit' and appears to have had no proof to hand that he was expected at Princeton. Not until the Seminary was contacted, and one of its staff actually sent to collect him, was he able to leave!

Such was the beginning, not of the expected two, but of forty years spent in the United States!

2

Princeton Theological Seminary,
1924–27

A T THE BEGINNING of the twentieth century the name of Princeton Theological Seminary was more highly revered in quiet corners of the Scottish Highlands than ever were the names of Oxford or Cambridge, and in many a croft volumes could be found written by some of the Christian teachers who had adorned that Seminary since its establishment in 1812. Through such books, and through well-known preachers who had visited Princeton or studied there, the Seminary had long been regarded as a centre of pure orthodoxy and piety. As late as the year 1912, when theological colleges in general were in full retreat from historic Christianity, the President of Princeton Seminary, Francis Landey Patton, could declare, 'The theological position of Princeton Seminary is exactly the same today that it was a hundred years ago.' For a hundred years she had 'simply taught the old Calvinistic Theology without modification'.

John Murray's first impressions of the Seminary are not known. Like many others who have passed from the crowded thorough-fares of New York into the beauty of rural New Jersey, where Princeton is situated, he would probably have been surprised by the charm of the Seminary's location and would have shared the enthusiasm of a student of an earlier day who wrote, 'The green fields, trees, birds, &c., are beyond all praise.'

On 30 September 1924, Princeton Seminary opened its one hundred and thirteenth session. The first events, as announced in the *Seminary Bulletin*, were 'the matriculation of new students in the parlor of Hodge Hall and the drawing for the choice of rooms by entering students at three o'clock in Stuart Hall'. The student accommodation, generally consisting of two rooms: a bedroom and a study, was divided between the original Alexander Hall, built of tan-coloured stone to the height of four floors, and the two more recent halls, Stuart and Brown. In all three the amenities had recently been improved. The *Bulletin* reported that during the summer 'bathrooms have been installed on the third floor of each of the three dormitories'. Probably John Murray was little concerned about the outcome of the ballot for rooms on that last day of September. His historic surroundings were full of new interests. We may be sure that he paid an early visit to the Seminary Library, with its 118,566 volumes, including the recently added 1,241 books which had been the property of the late Benjamin B. Warfield. He would also have explored the nearby University, with its original Nassau Hall building still standing from the 1750s, and the old graveyard beside Mercer Street, which contains the dust of Princeton's past leaders. The Scottish names on not a few of the tombstones in that quiet spot were reminders of the many who had made the same journey before him.

The student body this year was 225 strong, and Murray saw them gathered for the first time as the new session 'formally opened' with a service in the Miller Chapel on the morning of 1 October. The young congregation, which included seventy Juniors, united to sing

> Faith of our fathers, holy faith,
> We will be true to thee till death . . .

and listened to Dr Samuel M. Zwemer of Cairo speak on 'The Determining Factor in the Fight for Character'. If John was not already aware of it, the sight of that congregation would have convinced him that he was by no means the only student coming to Princeton from overseas. Seventeen could be counted from China and Korea, quite apart from other lands.[1]

Despite the apparent permanence of the Seminary's traditions, John Murray had arrived as Princeton was entering upon the most unsettled period in its long history, and even in Zwemer's opening address a trace of the cause of that unsettlement was observable. Of course, the famous missionary from Egypt was evangelical, and he pleaded for higher spiritual devotion, but amidst it all was a quotation from Harry Emerson Fosdick, a Baptist minister who was currently occupying the pulpit of the First Presbyterian Church, New York, and making no secret of his theological liberalism. Earlier that year, 1924, the subject of liberalism, and of Fosdick's liberalism in particular, had been before the General Assembly of the Presbyterian Church, yet without any effective action being taken. Zwemer probably shared in the denomination's growing belief that what was needed in the church was 'life' and 'practical Christianity' more than 'dogma'.

While there was no advocacy of liberalism within Princeton Seminary, there was already a division within the Faculty on the question of how the new views should be regarded. In fact, what was to prove a crucial turning point in the Seminary's history had already occurred in 1914 when Patton was succeeded in the presidency by the Rev. Dr J. Ross Stevenson. As a man of faith and prayer, there was much to be admired in Ross Stevenson, but his views on theological education revealed that he had no vision for the maintenance of the Seminary's distinctive position, and it became his increasing ambition that the Seminary, instead of

[1] The international influence of Princeton Seminary can be judged from the fact that in 1925 there were 3,011 alumni of the Seminary alive, including 80 in Britain, 47 in India, 80 in China, and 43 in Africa.

being in forthright opposition to liberal theology within the Presbyterian Church, should gain a reputation for representing a greater breadth of view. While support for Stevenson's viewpoint within the Faculty came from his friend Charles R. Erdman, Professor of Practical Theology since 1906, the majority of the teaching staff viewed the new attitude with dismay. B. B. Warfield had even ceased to attend Faculty meetings before his death in 1921. When that event occurred, J. Gresham Machen wrote to his mother, 'It seemed to me that the old Princeton – a great institution it was – died when Dr Warfield was carried out.'[1] Nonetheless, in 1924 Princeton Seminary still had the ablest Reformed teachers in the world. Caspar Wistar Hodge, Jr (1870-1937), grandson of Charles Hodge, having assisted Warfield for twenty years, had succeeded him as Professor of Theology. Geerhardus Vos (1862-1949) was Professor of Biblical Theology. Robert Dick Wilson (1856-1930) and Oswald T. Allis (1878-1973) were distinguished in the Old Testament field, with William Park Armstrong (1874-1944) and J. Gresham Machen (1881-1937) in the New. These men, and others of the Faculty, shared Machen's inability to believe 'that the faith which Warfield represented will ever really die'. As early as 1906, Vos had argued cogently against the modern depreciation of New Testament history and doctrine by those advocates who gave first place to 'life'. Redemption, he argued, is bound up with historical events and facts, and it is the doctrines of Scripture that give the meaning of those facts:

> To join in the outcry against dogma and fact means to lower the
> ideal of what the Christian consciousness ought normally to be to
> the level of the spiritual depression of our own day and generation.
> How much better that we should all strive to raise our drooping

---

[1] *J, Gresham Machen, A Biographical Memoir,* Ned B. Stonehouse (1955; repr. Edinburgh: Banner of Truth, 1987), p. 310.

faith and to re-enrich our depleted experience up to the standard of
those blessed periods in the life of the Church, when the belief in
Bible history and the religion of the heart went hand in hand and
kept equal pace, when people were ready to lay down their lives for
facts and doctrines, because facts and doctrines formed the daily
spiritual nourishment of their souls. May God by His Spirit maintain among us, and through our instrumentality revive around us,
that truly evangelical type of piety which not merely tolerates facts
and doctrines, but draws from them its strength and inspiration in
life and service, its only comfort and hope in the hour of death.[1]

It was this understanding of Christianity which H. E. Fosdick
was rejecting when he denied the virgin birth and other basic facts
and doctrines, as did the signatories of the Auburn Affirmation in
1924.[2]

That same year, the year of John Murray's arrival at Princeton,
the differing assessments of the need of the times within the
Seminary had become public knowledge. In this process the chief
catalyst was undoubtedly J. Gresham Machen, the Assistant Professor of New Testament, who, in the opinion of one of his pupils,
was, 'almost certainly the most effective teacher on the campus of
Princeton Theological Seminary in the middle 1920s'.[3] Aged forty-
three when Murray first saw him, Machen was already at the
centre of a growing controversy. In the preceding twelve months
Machen had been the stated supply at the First Presbyterian
Church of Princeton. In this period it had been headline news that
Dr Henry Van Dyke, a leading Presbyterian figure of liberal beliefs

---

[1] 'Christian Faith and the Truthfulness of Bible History', *The Princeton Theological Review*, 1906, pp. 289–305.

[2] The Auburn Affirmation was a statement, originally signed by 150 Presbyterian ministers in January 1924, which pleaded for liberty for different 'theories'
of belief within the Church.

[3] Paul Woolley, *The Significance of J. Gresham Machen Today*, 1977, p. 6.

in Princeton University, had given up his pew in that Church in protest over Machen's preaching. During 1924 there was also considerable controversy in the newspapers over Machen's latest book, the very title of which, *Christianity and Liberalism*,[1] was offensive to many. Earlier in the year, Machen had been succeeded in his supply post at the First Presbyterian Church by his colleague, Charles Erdman, whereupon Dr Van Dyke at once returned to his pew! Commentators in the press were not wrong when they concluded that a difference had come about between Machen and Erdman. Indeed, it became incontrovertible, for at the 1924 General Assembly of the Presbyterian Church, Machen chose to support the nomination of Clarence Edward Macartney rather than Erdman as Moderator. Macartney was known to share Machen's opposition to Fosdick's teaching.

Zwemer's quotation from Fosdick on that first October morning of the Seminary's 1924 session can hardly have been accidental. It was a straw in the wind of change. Ross Stevenson was certainly careful in the men he chose for these formal openings; but, though evangelicals, they were not representatives of the old order.

John Murray had been at Princeton for little more than a month when a visitor arrived who could speak with authority on what had once been the common outlook of the whole Faculty. During 3–7 November 1924, F. L. Patton, Stevenson's predecessor, delivered a series of five lectures. Though he had passed his eighty-second birthday 'the lecturer spoke with great vigour and maintained the deepest interest throughout'. Speaking on 'The New Christianity' Patton declared: 'It takes but limited experience and observation to note that the religious thought and activity of the present day are

---

[1] The book was published in February 1923. That year somewhat less than a thousand copies were sold, 'but,' writes Stonehouse, 'in 1924, as the book caught on and the controversy became even more intense, the total was nearly five thousand copies'. *J Gresham Machen*, p. 341.

different from that of 50 years ago . . . This different Christianity appears as a disease and as an epidemic.' Referring to historic Calvinism, he stated a conviction which some of his hearers delighted to remember in later years: 'I rejoice that it is a system so co-ordinated, whose doctrines are so concatenated, which has been so logically constructed, that if discovered in some future age by an excavating palaeontologist, he would be forced to remark: "Gentlemen, this belonged to the order of vertebrates."'[1]

In 1924 the Seminary still followed its original custom of providing no catering for students. From the beginning this had been supplied by homes around the Seminary, including, at one time, the home of a certain widowed Mrs Benham. By the beginning of the twentieth century the arrangement had given way to four eating clubs of which the most famous was 'the Benham'. Machen had called it 'the swellest' when he first joined it as a Junior in 1902, expressing his misgivings that it was 'too stuck up to be spiritually minded, or to have a good influence in the Seminary'. It would be interesting to know how John Murray came to be elected to the Benham Club and what he made of its traditions on his own admission. 'Officers' continued to enforce these traditions and every table was provided with a receptacle for fines which they might impose for any breach in the club's code. A fine of 25 cents, for example, could be levied for the failure of any member to amuse his fellow members with a humorous story when called upon to do so. Such 'stunting' was a regular part of the relaxation which followed meals. John, as a Junior, was soon put to the test and not a few were surprised to discover how the dour Scot proved quite equal to it.

Whether the incident took place at this time or later, Everett F. Harrison was later to recall one of John's escapes from fining:

---

[1] Quoted in *The Princeton Seminary Bulletin*, 1924.

He rose to the occasion by telling a story of an American tourist who was visiting Scotland. As his guide showed him one beauty spot after another, he acknowledged that they were worth seeing, but always insisted that there were spots just as beautiful back in the U.S.A. Finally, however, they came to a lovely loch that really entranced him and he blurted out, 'I wish we had that little lake back in the States.' His guide said, 'I am sure you can arrange it. You Americans can do almost anything, you know.' Said the tourist, 'But how could I do it?' 'It's really quite simple,' said the guide. 'You get a tube to connect with this loch and lay the tube under the Atlantic. Then when you get home, if you can suck as hard as you can blow, you will soon have our beautiful loch over there.' I have never forgotten the story or the uproar that followed (among the students) when John brought it to a conclusion.

Clarence W. Duff, a Junior with Murray in 1924 and subsequently a missionary to Ethiopia, retained this memory fifty years later:

Illustrative of John Murray's balanced humanity, I recall his prayers in our class prayer meetings, and his subtle Scottish wit during meals at old Benham Club where he held his own in lively jousts with Irish fellow-members. I do not mean to contrast these aspects of his personality, but think of them as complementing each other in his life as a Christian. I think I had never heard praying quite like that before, with its awesome sense of God's holiness and man's sinfulness and creaturehood, combined with full assurance of His love and grace, with much of the prayer expressed in the words of Scripture.

Alexander N. MacLeod, preparing for a life of mission work in the Far East, was first drawn to him as 'a quiet and studious fellow Scot'. Some of his old class-mates have also recalled their initial contact with him. David Freeman had his first conversation with

John following a lecture on Hymnody by Louis F. Benson. Murray's thoughtful comments, as they walked back to his room at the bottom of the staircase in Brown Hall, opened up new vistas to Freeman on the subject of Christian worship.

One young Irishman early caught Murray's attention. Although a year his senior, Jim Grier attended with him an optional course of lectures by Caspar Wistar Hodge on 'Imputation' and had the habit of pressing eagerly to the front to elicit more information from the professor once the class of about eighty was dismissed! Forty years later the two were still to be side by side in Christian endeavour.

Allan A. MacRae traces his first contact with Murray to a conversation with their Greek instructor:

Once when I was chatting with Dr Machen he spoke about a test he had just given in New Testament Textual Criticism and remarked that the paper he had received from a young Scot named John Murray was one of the finest test papers he had ever received. This whetted my interest. Soon John and I were taking occasional walks together in the countryside around Princeton. I was greatly impressed with his intellectual ability, but even more with his great devotion to Christ and his strong determination to stand by his convictions on every point, and equally pleased to find that this attitude was combined with a remarkable charity and love for other Christians, even when they differed with him on rather important points.

One aspect of Murray's character which soon impressed itself on others was his readiness to give encouragement. A classmate remembers calling at John's room in the endeavour to raise money for missionary work in Korea: 'He asked me what was being given on the average, and when I told him, he delved into his trunk and brought out some money, then handed me a sum in excess of the amount I had named. His comment was, "Perhaps some of the students may not be able to give as much as they would like to give.'"

Another fellow-student, Albert J. Sanders, later a missionary in the Philippines, recalls help of a different kind from Murray:

> On one occasion I was invited to preach in the Witherspoon Street Presbyterian Church, a 100 per cent black congregation [in Princeton, New Jersey]. Much to my surprise, at the close of the service I met John who had gone there to hear me preach. He gave me a real boost in spirit when quite calmly he remarked that he believed that God would use me fruitfully in the work of His kingdom. Somehow this word of encouragement from him meant more to me than perhaps from any other student.

Alexander MacLeod retained a similar memory:

> One evening at our 'practice preaching' session, I tried to preach on the theme, 'The Bible or Babel', expressing the thought that unless we agreed on accepting the Bible of Christ and His apostles as our standard of truth, the only alternative was theological confusion and chaos. Professor Smith who was in charge, in his critique after the sermon, severely took me to task for painting such a gloomy picture of the state of the Church. [It was about the time of the Fosdick controversy.] After the class was dismissed, John Murray and Ned Stonehouse came up to me with words of encouragement, saying that they agreed with me in my assertions; only, John added the suggestion that my argument in my sermon was a little too much utilitarian (in contrast to being theological or biblical). I have never forgotten how much their encouragement meant to me after the thorough scolding I got before the whole class!

It was John Murray's habit to keep few of the letters he received, but a notable exception was correspondence that came from his father while he was at Princeton. In later years a missionary friend in far-off Africa who had formerly shared fully in the hospitality and rich fellowship of John Murray's home, once exclaimed to him in a letter, 'Ah, Badbea! The mouth of my soul waters.' No one knew that feeling more deeply than John, and a few carefully folded letters from his father, which have survived the passage of time, give glimpses of how the family circle also felt his absence. On four sides of paper well filled with items of news, Alexander Murray begins and ends a letter as follows:

> Badbea,
> Bonar Bridge.
> 3 Feb. 1925

My Dear Son,

We have just received your letter this evening; it took 14 days to reach here; you wrote on 17th January. We are always so glad to see that your health is keeping so well although sorry to know that your eye is weak at times. Of course, it is too much strain owing to the work. I trust you will not overdo the eye although the work is necessary.

Willie is ploughing in these days. We are very far behind with the work this year as we had a very wet winter, the wettest anyone here remembers, and scarcely any frost . . .

Mr Gray, Lairg, is very poorly since two months ago. I was saying to him that I hoped the Lord would spare him on earth until a minister would be set over these poor parishes, but I may be taken away myself and him left. Indeed if I will be left behind him he will be missed as he is a man of ballast and sense along with grace. I am missing poor Johie very much. I did not expect one day that she would leave home, poor lassie, but times have changed. I trust the ever Blessed One will give health and strength to her and bless her with spiritual blessings in Christ Jesus!

Many thanks for being so mindful in writing home; I trust it will be for the Lord's glory you being there.

Your loving father,
Alexr. Murray

The first year at Princeton ended early in May 1925, and new experiences followed as John took the train west to Detroit. Writing from there to a correspondent in Australia, on 19 May, he commented, 'My session's work at Princeton I enjoyed very much. It is a great matter to have an institution with such scholarship still faithful to the truth and faith once and for all delivered to the saints.'

The visit to Detroit, and the further journey into Canada which followed, require some explanation, not least because they had an important bearing on decisions which were to change the course of his life. For over a century Canada had become a new home for many emigrant Scots, of whom not a few had been reared under the sound of the gospel. It was to such people in Ontario, that Robert Murray M'Cheyne's friend, William Chalmers Burns, had gone to minister in the 1840s. At the end of the nineteenth century, Scots in Canada who sympathized with the stand taken at home by the Free Presbyterian Church, had begun to organize congregations and mission charges under the same name. Around 1925, several thousand Scots were still emigrating to Canada each year and the Free Presbyterian Synod of that year reported the anticipation that 'the Church would greatly increase, especially in the West'. The principal hindrance, it was considered, was the lack of ministers to pastor the congregations which were being brought together, and one argument for John Murray's course at Princeton was that, in his vacations, he might supply some of the stations in Canada and the United States.

Detroit was probably John Murray's first experience of one of these congregations of exiled Highlanders, and he prized their friendship no less than they prized his preaching. The high wages paid by the automobile industry in Detroit had drawn Scots from Canada, including not a few who had crossed from the Isle of Lewis as recently as 1922. A Free Presbyterian deputy reported: 'This city is growing enormously every year, and is already bigger in numbers than the city of Glasgow, and covers a much bigger area. The Ford Motor Works alone employs over 100,000 in Detroit itself.'

From Detroit, Murray journeyed to Winnipeg, the gateway to the great wheat prairies of the West and the Canadian rail-centre midway between the Atlantic and the Pacific. Of this visit it was subsequently reported in the *Free Presbyterian Magazine*, 'The congregation highly appreciated his services and the numbers increased while he was there.' Perhaps it was in part due to this encouragement that the Winnipeg congregation were able to open their own building the following year.

It may well have been in the summer of 1925 that John Murray was also able to pay the first of innumerable subsequent visits to Chesley, Ontario, where the Free Presbyterian congregation, along with a neighbouring congregation at Lochalsh, enjoyed the ministry of the Rev. William Matheson. When John Murray preached at Mr Matheson's funeral some thirty years later, he was to describe him as the best friend he had on earth outside his own family.

We have little information on the remainder of John Murray's three years at Princeton Seminary to May 1927, when the degrees of Bachelor and Master of Theology were conferred upon him. Before that date differences within both the Faculty and the student body itself had further polarized. In 1925, C. R. Erdman denied that there were any doctrinal differences within the Seminary, claiming that disagreement was only over 'spirit' and 'methods', and virtually blamed Machen for 'bitterness and intolerance'. Replying in the columns of *The Presbyterian*, Machen asserted that this was not a true representation of the case. His 'high personal esteem' for Dr Erdman did not affect his conviction that a considerable difference existed, not, indeed, over any particular belief, but over the place of *belief* itself:

> Dr Erdman does not indeed reject the doctrinal system of our church, but he is perfectly willing to make common cause with those who reject it, and he is perfectly willing on many occasions to keep it in the background. I, on the other hand, can never consent to keep it in the background. Christian doctrine, I hold, is not merely connected with the gospel, but it is identical with the gospel, and if I did not preach it at all times, and especially in those places where it subjects me to personal abuse, I should regard myself as guilty of sheer unfaithfulness to Christ.[1]

In 1926 the Seminary Faculty elected Machen as Professor of Apologetics but, in the same year, advised by Erdman and Ross Stevenson, the General Assembly of the Presbyterian Church (for the first time in the Seminary's history) declined to confirm the Faculty's act and decided on postponing their decision until an investigating committee could examine the unsettled state of the Seminary. Excitement was running high when F. B. Meyer gave the opening address at the commencement of Murray's last year in September 1926. Meyer, a prominent English Baptist pastor who had failed to give any support to Spurgeon in the Downgrade

[1] *J. Gresham Machen*, p. 376. Stonehouse's work on Machen is one of the most important Christian biographies of the twentieth century and is invaluable for its interpretation of this period.

controversy, was of the same general outlook as Stevenson, and his weak address included an exhortation that the prospective preachers before him should 'soak in Wordsworth'. That same term commenced with the Faculty taking the unprecedented step of censuring President Stevenson for his part in the General Assembly's action concerning the Seminary. Nonetheless, the committee appointed by the Assembly began its hearings at Princeton in November, and by April 1927 its recommendations pointed to the likelihood of a reorganization of the Seminary, so that the balance of power might shift against those who stood for the institution's traditional doctrinal position.

Tension of this kind inevitably affected the student body. The Students' Association at Princeton Seminary had long belonged to the Middle Atlantic Association of Theological Seminaries, but during the year 1924–5, representatives had been so disturbed by the liberalism which they found at a Conference of the Association convened at Drew Theological Seminary that, after much debate, the Association withdrew from the connection and joined with the students of five other theological institutions to form a new fellowship named the League of Evangelical Students. While Stevenson and Erdman clearly disapproved of this step, and the more exclusive position taken up by the League, Machen and the majority of the Faculty were encouraged. In an Introduction to his book, *What Is Faith?*, published in November 1925, Machen wrote thus of what they were then witnessing at the Seminary:

> The morale of our theological student body during the past years had been becoming rather low; there was marked indifference to the central things of the faith; and religious experience was of the most superficial kind. But during the academic year, 1924–25, there has been something like an awakening. Youth has begun to think for itself; the evil of compromising associations has been discovered;

Christian heroism in the face of opposition has come again to its rights . . . Controversy, in other words, has resulted in a striking intellectual and spiritual advance. Some of us discern in all this the work of the Spirit of God . . . It is out of such times of questioning that great revivals come. God grant that it may be so today![1]

It is clear that John Murray was one of the most earnest supporters of the League of Evangelical Students. While not all the Seminary students shared in the League's stand,[2] the number of prize-winning students among those who did so was noticeable. Two of the latter in particular were to be Murray's friends for life. They were Cornelius Van Til, who wrote a prize-winning paper in his Senior year, and David Freeman, who took 'the first A. A. Hodge Prize in Systematic Theology'. Murray himself won the Gelston-Winthrop Fellowship in Systematic Theology. The *Seminary Bulletin* was later to report, 'Few students have maintained as high a level of scholarship as did Mr Murray during his Seminary course.'

Without question John Murray's years at Princeton exercised a formative influence upon his whole life and thought. It was not that his spiritual life and outlook were changed; these had already been decided in that school of Christian godliness which he had been privileged to know from his youth in his native Scotland. But that school, for all its lingering fragrance of brighter days, lacked outstanding mentors in theology. For instruction it depended chiefly upon the Puritan divines of an earlier age. At Princeton, however, Murray found the theology of the *Westminster Confession of Faith* in living embodiment, and taught from the original languages of the Scriptures with a freshness and an exactness of

---

[1] *What is Faith?* (1925; repr. Edinburgh: Banner of Truth, 1991), p. 42.

[2] The student vote for joining the League of Evangelical Students was 140 for, and 70 against.

exegesis which was new to him. Before he crossed the Atlantic he
had known little Greek; it was the Seminary, and perhaps the
instruction of Geerhardus Vos in particular,[1] which instilled in him
the conviction that doctrine must be arrived at through a pains-
taking examination of the Scriptures in their original languages.
While the Puritans themselves held that view, the greater exegetical precision of the more modern commentators was scarcely
known to them.[2] At Princeton, then, Murray's commitment to the
Reformed Faith was not changed, but it became, in a new way,
rooted in the Bible itself.

The following letter to his former instructor in Greek, written
nearly a year after he had left the Seminary, conveys something of
what the Seminary had meant to him:

Badbea,
Bonar Bridge,
Sutherland,
Scotland
April 2nd, 1928

Dear Dr Machen,

Seeing that another Session of work at Princeton is drawing near a
close, I consider that I ought to pen a few lines to you. It is with
consciousness of fault that I do so, because a letter was owing long
ago. My failure in this respect, however, is by no means to be
regarded as the measure of my affection for you or for Princeton.
Absent in body, I am frequently present in spirit. My mind gravi-
tates to Princeton as it does to home. With all my heart I hope you

---

[1] Commending the British Edition of Vos's *Biblical Theology* in 1974, he spoke
of the author as 'the most penetrating exegete it has been my privilege to know'.
[2] For this reason, while it was Murray's life-long practice to recommend
Puritan authors, he did not generally commend their commentaries.

are well in health and that out of the abundance of the grace that is in Jesus Christ you are being strengthened with all might by His Spirit in the inner man. I have been receiving bits of information regarding Princeton, and am keeping up with developments in connection with its re-organization, through the pages of *The Presbyterian*. There will no doubt be under-currents and phases of the controversy, which is so vital to our faith and Presbyterian heritage, that will not reach the North of Scotland, but I presume that *The Presbyterian* will keep us fairly well informed. I wonder very much if there is any reaction probable owing to the diffusion of more accurate information? It was with pleasure that I read your pamphlet, 'A Plea for Fair Play'. I suppose that if Princeton's historical identity should be undermined and destroyed there are sufficient in America loyal enough to the Reformed faith who would do their utmost to found and build another to take its place, but the library could not possibly be duplicated.

The unusually large attendance of students this year would no doubt have given you an uplift. I would be interested to know how the League of Evangelical Students is faring in the campus and in the College in general. I have had no information along this line. Messrs Rian, Woodbridge and Macrae are greatly enjoying this winter in Berlin. They are courageously and effectively facing the current of naturalistic criticism.

It was with a certain amount of apprehensiveness that I learned recently of the ill-health of Dr Vos. We can only hope that he will yet be spared for some time for further usefulness in the church of Christ. His praise is in all the churches. Without question, through him as instrument, God's truth went into all the earth. With regard to the future of Princeton we may look upon the outlook as dark, but there is the truth which we ought never to let slip from our minds and which ought to bear us up in the strain and stress of discouragement and apparent failure, that the cause of Christ, with all that this means for the church and a lost world, will assuredly triumph. 'Thou shalt arise and have mercy upon Zion, for the time to favour her, yea, the set time is come.' 'God is our refuge and our strength, a very present help in time of trouble.' Christ will reign until all his enemies will be made his footstool. In the midst of trial, persecution and temptations we must be ambitious to repeat the endurance of Job: 'He knoweth the way that I take; when he hath tried me I shall come forth as gold. My foot hath held his steps, his way have I kept and not declined. Neither have I gone back from the commandment of his lips; I have esteemed the words of his mouth more than my necessary food.'

I hope you enjoyed your tour in the British Isles last summer and that you met with a warm reception. Indirectly I got to know a little of your movements. Of course you had returned before I landed on this side.

I must draw to a close. Please convey my heartiest greetings to Dr Armstrong. When you find it convenient I should be delighted for a few lines from you. Accept my warmest regards, while I remain,

Yours affectionately,
John Murray

This letter meant so much to Machen, as he read it in his study on the fourth floor of Alexander Hall, that it survives among his papers to this day.

He also wrote at once to Dr Vos, passing on news from the letter and professing to his colleague, 'I do feel that the service of real students like John Murray makes our life at Princeton worth while.' His reply to Murray reads as follows:

April 16th 1928

Dear Mr Murray,

Your letter of April 2nd has brought refreshment to my soul in the midst of a very distressing time. No gift of God is more precious to us in these days than the sympathy of friends like you, who really know what issues are involved, but who at the same time find comfort and strength where alone they can be found, in the great and precious promises of God.

Your presence added greatly to Princeton Seminary when you were here. I do not suppose that you know fully how important and how salutary was your influence in the student body. If we of the Faculty have been able to serve in any measure men like you, then Princeton has not altogether been without use in the world; and even though the institution now perishes, its work will remain.

The League of Evangelical Students is very fortunate in having secured – apparently the thing is practically settled – the services of Paul Woolley as General Secretary, to travel throughout the country and otherwise to carry on the business of the League, for next year. Mr Woolley returned from his studies in Germany greatly broadened in his outlook and at the same time greatly strengthened in his own Christian convictions. He is intending to go to China, but conditions there for the moment are rather unfavorable, and I think that he has definitely decided to take up the work of the League. The services of such a man were sorely needed.

In the student body of Princeton Seminary the situation, as shown by the recent election of officers for next year, is satisfactory to about the same degree as that which has prevailed for some years past. Philip Austin, the conservative candidate for President, was elected by almost a two-thirds majority – just about the same majority as that which has prevailed in similar issues for two or three years.

In the Church at large, I think that our cause is increasing in favor – the cause of the present management of Princeton Seminary, I mean. If those who are charged with responsibility at the center, the majority group of directors, will stand absolutely firm, avoiding the deadly notion of compromise, it is possible that we may win in the General Assembly in May. But of course the battle is very sore.

I love to think of you as being engaged in the true work of preaching the Gospel. Write to me when you find time.

Cordially yours,
J. Gresham Machen

3

By Paths Not Known

IT WAS CHARACTERISTIC of John Murray's reticence that in his letter to Machen of April 1928 he said nothing of a great trial through which he was then passing. No one doubted that when he left Princeton he would soon be called to a pastoral charge in his own denomination in Scotland. While at Seminary he stood out among his contemporaries as a preacher. Jim Grier remembered how he earned the unusual distinction of receiving a visit in his room from President Ross Stevenson, following a sermon he had preached in a homiletics class. On such occasions comment was expected from the listening professor and students, but Stevenson's action on this occasion was not known to have a precedent. There was good reason, then, why Machen could 'love to think' of him preaching the gospel. Yet the surprising fact is that when Machen's letter arrived at Badbea his former pupil had not been in a pulpit for several months! Behind Murray's cessation from preaching lay events which changed the course of his whole future life.

Despite John's eagerness to return home after three years away, he had supplied the Free Presbyterian congregation in Detroit in the early summer of 1927 and had not recrossed the Atlantic until the end of June. Once back in the Highlands of Scotland he took up various invitations to preach from Free Presbyterian charges. At the beginning of September he was in Inverness, where he remained for over a month, supplying the congregation of his denomination which then met at North Church Place. For many Sundays in that autumn of 1927 he also served the vacant joint-charges of Dingwall and Beauly, and such was the spiritual liberty which he found in these congregations that he began to wonder if this was not the flock which he was intended to serve. It is still remembered in Dingwall how the congregation increased in those memorable weeks and how the services 'attracted young people, and were veritable gospel feasts to older Christians'. From the latter class, as one hearer recalls, 'special mention might be made of three elderly ladies, choice Christians, who could fit well into Bunyan's portrayal of Prudence, Piety and Charity. They loved "Johnnie Murray", as they affectionately called him, and his preaching was to them as "wine on the lees well refined".'

At this juncture it seemed that John's ordination would soon follow and as a matter of course. The *Free Presbyterian Magazine* reported the conclusion of his theological course and the expectation that, along with Messrs D. Urquhart and Robert Sinclair, he would be taken on trial for licence. In subsequent issues of the magazine, reference is made to the ordination of Urquhart and Sinclair, but henceforth John Murray's name virtually disappears from the recorded history of the denomination. The truth is that by the end of 1927 action had been taken against his being given any further preaching duties, and at once all his opportunities at Dingwall and elsewhere were at an end.

Behind this act of discipline lay a controversy on the use of the Lord's Day. Strange as it must be to those who read Murray's writings on the permanence of the Fourth Commandment, and stranger still to those who knew his personal care to honour that command, the charge which led to his being silenced was that of laxity respecting the Christian Sabbath. Murray's general position on the use of Sunday was well stated at this time in what was possibly his first published letter. Addressed to the Editor of the *Inverness Courier*, who published it under the title 'Sunday Excursions', it read as follows:

SUNDAY EXCURSIONS

To the Editor of the *Inverness Courier*

30 Broadstone Park,

Inverness, September 1st, 1927

Sir, – A contribution to the 'concerted action on the part of Christian people with a view to the defence of the Lord's Day' desired by the Rev. Principal Macleod, may perhaps be granted space in your columns. One is reminded of the Scripture, 'Curse ye Meroz, said the angel of the LORD, curse ye bitterly the inhabitants thereof; because they came not to the help of the LORD, to the help of the LORD against the mighty.'

The plea for liberty in the matter of scripture precept is a current and plausible argument. We must concede that liberty is a God-given and inalienable right and privilege of man. We further concede that scriptural principles are not to be applied by the imposition of arbitrary and mechanical rules. But liberty is never to be defined in terms of licence. Liberty, to be worthy of the name, is always delimited by law. Liberty without law is licentiousness and anarchy. Law without moral freedom is soulless necessity. In this precise question, what is the law within which our liberty is secured, and without which our liberty is lost? In holy writ its first intimation occurs in Genesis 2, 2–3. 'And on the seventh day God ended His work which He had made. And He rested on the seventh day from all His works which He had made. And God blessed the seventh day and sanctified it, because that in it He had rested from all His work which God created and made.' The principle of God's moral government and of man's nature as created in the image of

God herein enunciated is the succession of six days' labour and one day of holy rest. This institution is not the provision of fallen humanity, but belongs to man as man. It has behind it the authority, wisdom and goodness of the Almighty Creator.

Commentary comes from the mouth of no less an authority than the Lord Jesus Himself: 'The Sabbath was made for man and not man for the Sabbath. Therefore the Son of man is Lord also of the Sabbath.' It was made by God for man as man. Christ is the Lord of the Sabbath and it is to His authority we must bow. Does this give any liberty to unmake the Sabbath, or too arbitrarily to interpret its meaning and character? To what did Christ make reference when he spoke of the Sabbath that was made and to which He sets indelibly the seal of His sanction and approval? Verily to the original institution as practically elucidated by the fourth commandment. The decalogue is not ceremonial. It is moral and therefore contains moral principles which are universal and perpetual in their obligation and application. The fourth word or commandment means that there is to be one day of holy rest following six days of labour. Two ideas belong to the essence of this law: separateness and holiness. One day in seven is to be different from the other six. It is to be separated. But the nature of its separation is also specified. It is not separation to sloth, or idleness or pleasure or recreation; it is separation unto the specific worship of God. There is one day in seven of cessation from the secular toils and cares, in order that man may without distraction devote himself to the meditation, contemplation and worship of God. This, Christ says, was made for man. Those who protested against excursions on the Lord's day realise that by these encroachments the honour and authority of God is assailed and that the central principles of the Sabbath law are at stake. Let not those who are out of sympathy with such a protest think that this is an attempt to perpetuate merely human traditions. There is a principle of God's moral government involved and the contraventions complained of are directly and unashamedly a breach of loyalty to Him whom we acknowledge and confess as our Master and Lord. The Son of Man is Lord also of the Sabbath.

Yours etc.,
John Murray

This letter, however, does not deal with the particular controversy which had arisen within Murray's own denomination. Concerned at the danger of a lowering of standards among church members, the Synod of the Free Presbyterian Church had ruled that members who used public transport ran 'in systematic disregard of the sacred day' and should be debarred from attendance at the Lord's Table. Controversy over this began in Canada in the summer of 1926 when William Matheson failed to uphold the Synod's ruling. As the appointed deputy of the Free Presbyterian Church, Matheson had gone to Winnipeg to open the new church building, but at the same time, as subsequently reported in the supreme court of his Church, 'he admitted to the Lord's Table and Baptism at Winnipeg parties debarred by findings of this Synod' – that is to say, people who used public transport for any reason on Sundays. Matheson did not himself use public transport on Sundays, but he considered that where persons could not get to church without the use of such transport there were no grounds for enforcing discipline and the suspension of privileges. It could not be assumed that the motive in such persons was disregard for the Sabbath, for the motive might well be concern to be present at the public means of grace. Did not the argument of 'necessity and mercy' hold in such cases? The Synod, thus questioned on their earlier ruling, held that no exceptions were allowable, and that Mr Matheson and his Kirk Session, if they persisted in their opinion, would not be considered a Kirk Session of the Free Presbyterian Church of Scotland.

When Murray returned to Scotland in the summer of 1927 the dispute was still at the stage of private correspondence between the minister of Chesley and one of the committees of the Free Presbyterian Church, but as Murray's close association with the Canadian congregations was well known, it was inevitable that his view on the matter should be ascertained. His position was indeed the same as Matheson's. Although unable himself to use public transport in good conscience on the Lord's Day, he believed that it was going beyond the authority of Scripture, to turn away from the Lord's Table someone who gave evidence of love to Christ, solely because they had used a tram to make their attendance possible. Free Presbyterian friends, forseeing that if he retained this belief he would be excluded from any office in the Church of his childhood, urged him to accept the Synod's ruling. It was clear, however, to John Murray, notwithstanding the pleas and reasoning of friends, that he could only uphold the discipline required by the Synod at the price of disobedience to his own conscience.

With a heavy heart he had to face the probability that his hopes of usefulness in the pastoral ministry of the Free Presbyterian Church would not now be realized. The way in which he had believed he was being led had suddenly, to all appearances, become a *cul-de-sac*. So any pleasure that he had in returning to farm work at Badbea in 1927 was tempered by the fact that after eight years of study for the ministry the goal was not even in sight! It is not hard to imagine what kind of a blow this was to his parents, and especially to his father, now well into his seventies, who had long been burdened by the need for more ministers in the North.

Apart from the farm work at home, there was only one avenue open to him. During his last year at Princeton he had won a Gelston-Winthrop Fellowship, which would support him, if he wished, in further studies. That was not his intention, for the pastoral office was what he most desired, but when that way was closed he decided to use the Fellowship award in theological studies at New College, Edinburgh.

Accordingly, in the summer of 1928, he took up lodging in the home of relatives, Mr and Mrs Harry Rattray, who lived at 14 George IV Bridge, Edinburgh, with their two daughters and son. Mrs Rattray was a first cousin of John's and during his time in Edinburgh she played the part of both a sister and a mother. Perhaps it was in the latter role that she asked him one day why he did not join the Free Church of Scotland instead of so faithfully maintaining his membership with the Free Presbyterians: after all, the Free Church, greatly reduced in numbers, had been purged of its liberal and Arminian elements in 1900 when the majority had joined with the United Presbyterians. John replied that he could not accept what he considered to be the lax manner in which the privilege of baptism was too often given in the Free Church, nor was it right to him for a Church to allow Freemasons within its membership. There the matter rested; he was glad to accompany the Rattrays to their Free Church congregation when services did not coincide with those in his own, but he could not see the Free Church ministry as a way out of his problem.

In the meantime, uncongenial though New College was in certain respects (it was no longer a Free Church College and no longer upheld the faith of the men who built it), he applied himself to Historical Theology. His written work included a thesis on 'Luther: His Doctrine of Atonement and His Relation to John Gerson.' Janet Rattray, now Mrs Macpherson, was in her first year in the University. She remembered John as a quiet and studious companion with whom she burned 'midnight-oil' over their respective books. In addition to theology, John was studying the Berlitz German course.

Mrs MacPherson particularly remembered the evening when John shared with her the decision he was taking which would so greatly change the course of his life. Some days before, a communication, postmarked Princeton, had arrived addressed to him. To his surprise it contained an invitation from Caspar Wistar Hodge to be his assistant in Systematic Theology, commencing in the fall of 1929. Without doubt there was an immediate, strong appeal in the proposal, yet the decision was not easy. Murray's heart was in Scotland, his parents were aged (his mother died in 1933), and he had no inclination to join the denomination to which Princeton Seminary belonged, namely the Presbyterian Church in the U.S.A. Besides, his objective was the pastorate, not a theological institution. And yet no other opportunities for usefulness were open to him. So the same night upon which he revealed the matter to his fellow-student, in the early summer of 1929, he slipped out of the house a little after midnight to despatch a cheap-rate cable to Hodge from the General Post Office in Princes Street. It was an unusual hour to be about the streets, and he thought it necessary to tell Janet, 'If your mother should hear me going out you can explain I have gone to send a cable to America, but don't tell her what it is!' It was, in fact, an acceptance of the call to Princeton, but with the proviso that he could only promise one year's service.

One practical difficulty which almost prevented his going was remembered by Allan MacRae:

John told me that when he was invited to teach in Princeton he immediately went to the American consulate in Edinburgh to ask for an immigrant visa, and was informed that the quota had already been filled for ten years to come. If he would leave his name they would put him on the list so that he could migrate to America eight years later. Although this seemed to make teaching in America impossible, he delayed a few days in sending a letter declining the offered position. In the meantime he visited a friend in Edinburgh and mentioned his disappointment to him. The friend suggested that they make inquiry at the office of the American consul in Glasgow. When John told this official of his desire to go to America he said: 'Yes, I can give you a visa immediately. By American law Scotland is limited to a certain number of immigrants each year. Edinburgh's quota may be full, but we still have vacancies, even for the present year.'

It was a changed Princeton Seminary to which John Murray returned in September 1929. For three years the struggle between the President, J. Ross Stevenson, and the majority of the Faculty had continued, with the Board of Directors (who controlled the administration of the Seminary) supporting the majority. But the majority were by this time very much a minority in the Presbyterian Church as a whole, where the opinion was now widespread that exponents of 'moderate theological liberalism' ought to have a place in the Church's life and thought. Each year support weakened for the conviction that liberalism and Christianity represented two different religions, and those who, like Machen continued to speak for that conviction were branded as uncharitable and isolationist. Thus the *Presbyterian Banner* criticized the Seminary's majority in these terms: 'Princeton may be standing where the Presbyterian Church stood in 1870, but not so the Church itself . . . If Princeton is standing where the Church stood in 1870, it is true that it should move forward and stand where the Church stands today.'

The committee appointed by the 1926 General Assembly to investigate conditions at Princeton had found that the Seminary did not intend to 'move', and consequently, to ensure that it did, the drastic proposal was made that the Seminary should be reorganized under a new board of control. Machen rightly judged the intention when he protested that, if such reorganization were carried through, 'the only men who will be tolerated in the Faculty will be men who hold a complacent view of the state of the Church'. At the 1928 General Assembly the proposal for reorganization was postponed, perhaps in part due to a petition (supported by 11,000 signatures) which claimed:

> The present Faculty carries on the best traditions of the Alexanders and the Hodges, of Green, Warfield and Patton. The only offence laid to the charge either of the Faculty or of the Board of Directors is excess of zeal for the purity of the faith. Is this a time when such a change can safely be entertained by the Church?

The General Assembly of 1929, however, was prepared to wait no longer. The reorganization of Princeton Seminary was carried through and among members of the new board were two who had signed and supported the liberalism of the Auburn Affirmation! Before the motion was carried, Machen was given but five minutes in which to argue for the last time that the proposed changes would remove Princeton from its historic biblical foundations. 'According to one account', writes Lefferts Loetscher, '"many listened to this contention with wondering incredulity".' They had no comprehension of what Machen meant by the testimony with which he concluded his all-too-brief speech: 'One thing at least is clear: there are many Christians in many lands who will feel that if the old Princeton goes, a light will have gone out of their lives.'

John Murray had accepted the invitation to Princeton before he knew of the fateful decision of the General Assembly which had met towards the end of May. But in view of the known uncertainty, as we have already seen, he had taken the precaution of adding the proviso that he could only promise one year's service. The wisdom of that condition was soon to be apparent. He found several of the upholders of the old theology still in the classrooms, notably

Caspar Wistar Hodge, Geerhardus Vos, and W. P. Armstrong, but
the changes in the Faculty were far-reaching. William Brenton
Greene, whom Machen referred to as 'one of the best Christians I
have ever known', had died in 1929. And, following the General
Assembly decision of 1929, three of the Seminary's leading professors, Oswald T. Allis, Robert Dick Wilson, and Machen himself
had resigned, followed by the young Cornelius Van Til, who only
that Spring had been appointed to the chair of Apologetics.

In July 1929 these three senior professors, supported by an
influential number of Presbyterian ministers, had determined to
commence another Seminary which would continue to supply
men for the ministry of their church and stand by the faith which
the old Princeton had so long proclaimed: 'the majesty and sovereignty of Almighty God, the total inability of fallen man to save
himself, and that the whole of salvation is to be ascribed to the
power and grace of God'. Thus it was that on 25 September 1929,
in Philadelphia, Westminster Theological Seminary began its
history.

The real change at Princeton was to take years to work out. In
the Fall of 1929, with 177 students (over against 50 at Westminster),
the Seminary remained numerically strong, but there was already
a difference of mood. The senior colleagues on the Faculty whom
Murray most respected remained in a mood of resignation to the
inevitable rather than with any enthusiasm for the future; as the
wife of one of them was known to say, 'It was very difficult to work
for one institution and pray for another.' They remained in close
friendship with their former colleagues who had moved to Philadelphia.

Practically nothing is known of Murray's teaching year at
Princeton. The *Princeton Seminary Bulletin* had noted his addition
to the Faculty with the comment, already noted above, 'Few
students have maintained as high a level of scholarship as did Mr

Murray during his Seminary course.' Undoubtedly he gave himself to the new work with his customary diligence, and with another quality noted by Cornelius Van Til: 'Humble boldness marked John's every doing, no less when he was known throughout the world as the greatest living Calvin scholar, than when he first began his career of teaching as an instructor at Princeton.' The remark of his friend, Ned B. Stonehouse, that he 'did not find the atmosphere in the reorganized Princeton congenial' is understandable. There was no escaping the conclusion that a battle had been fought and lost, and he also knew that the front line of the wider battle was now in Philadelphia with Machen. Somehow, despite all his labours, Machen still continued to write for publication and in March 1930 he did not forget to send John Murray his latest (and largest) work as soon as it was published. The gift brought the following response:

309 Alexander Hall

Princeton, N.J.

17 March 1930

My Dear Dr Machen,

I presume that you are responsible for my receiving just the other day from Harper Brothers your new book on the Virgin Birth of Christ. I wish to thank you very cordially. I cannot express my appreciation of your mindfulness and kindness. I do very highly esteem the gift and shall look forward to my making a careful perusal of it when time permits. You have without question put the church under a great debt, for there was certainly required a scholarly and frank discussion of the evidence on which our belief in this article of our faith rests and many, I believe, will now rejoice that such is in our hands. I am sometimes very much surprised in finding how subtly disbelief in the Virgin Birth has taken hold of those who in other respects could be called evangelical. Surely it is the manifestation of a naturalistic temper of mind that sets the wisdom of man above the wisdom of God.

I do hope that, in the midst of the tribulations which you have in common with all the people of God, you are also enjoying much of the consolations of the gospel of peace. 'I am persuaded, that neither death, nor life, nor angels, nor principalities, nor powers, nor things present, nor things to come, nor height, nor depth, nor any other creature, shall be able to separate us from the love of God, which is in Christ Jesus our Lord.'

I am sorry that Dr Hodge is not so well. We do hope that he may recover in due time.

With my kindest regards and best wishes,

I remain, with hearty thanks,

Very sincerely your Friend,
John Murray

A few months later Machen was in touch with Murray again, this time with a request which was to prove a turning point in Murray's life. Of all the Faculty appointments in the new Seminary at Philadelphia, the department of Systematic Theology had proved the most difficult to fill. Stonehouse observes: 'It is an illuminating commentary on the theological competence of the ministry, that Machen and his associates did not know where to turn within the Presbyterian Church in the U.S.A., to find a man for this chair of genuine scholarly attainments and of undoubted understanding of, and commitment to, the Reformed Faith.' At length the problem was deferred, as Dr R. B. Kuiper promised to fill the gap by teaching Theology for one year. The solution which the Westminster Faculty finally proposed is best stated in the following historic letter of Machen's:

Westminster Theological Seminary,
Philadelphia,
June 25, 1930

Dear Mr Murray:

It is quite needless to say that our Faculty, when it met last Friday, voted unanimously and most heartily to nominate you to the Board of Trustees as for the position of Instructor in Systematic Theology for next year. The three absent members of the Faculty, who were communicated with by telegram, concurred heartily in the action.

It seems impracticable to call a meeting of the Board of Trustees, indeed there might be difficulty in securing a quorum, but Dr Frank H. Stevenson, the President of the Board, is consulting every individual member by letter. There can be no doubt but that the Board will concur in the Faculty's action. If, in accordance with what you told me the other day, you desire to have some official communication as the basis of your consultation with your presbytery in Scotland, you can wait until you hear from Dr Stevenson. The Faculty hesitated about communicating to you officially an action which should be reported first to the Board of Trustees, since such procedure might constitute a bad precedent. But of course all such questions of procedure are in the present case of little importance. The really important thing is that we have a very urgent need of you in a work which I know that you as well as we believe to be the Lord's work. I cannot bear to think of even the possibility of our failing to have you next year.

Because of the irregularity of the present situation, when no formal meeting of the Board is possible, and above all because of our doubt whether you would be willing at the present moment to form a definitely permanent connection with our institution, we put our action in the form indicated above. But for myself, and I think

I speak also for every one of the others, I may say that it is my strong conviction, as well as my earnest hope, that you will find Westminster Seminary to offer you the best possible field of service and that an engagement which just for the moment is only for one year may only be the preliminary step to something of a (technically) more permanent kind. However, you must not let any decision about that matter trouble you for the moment. We have asked for your services in a great emergency, and we could not do without you without very serious loss and peril to the institution that we serve.

Paul Woolley was unable to find you when he was in Princeton on Monday evening, since the painters were in possession of your room, and no one of whom inquiry could have been made was at hand.

Cordially yours,
J. Gresham Machen

Machen's reference to Murray's consultation with his 'presbytery in Scotland' requires explanation. The controversy between William Matheson and the Free Presbyterian Synod had concluded in 1930 with the expulsion of Matheson (and the members and adherents of his congregations in Ontario) from the parent denomination. But officially, although debarred from preaching, as already noted, John Murray remained a 'divinity student' of the Free Presbyterian Church and, despite all that had happened, he probably still felt an obligation to help train men for the ministry back in Scotland were that to become possible. A permanent emigration to North America had never been his intention. Accordingly, it seems that in the Spring of 1930, before he received the invitation from Westminster, he had asked for a clarification of his position from the Northern Presbytery, to which his home congregation at Bonar Bridge belonged. The Presbytery had evidently felt themselves unable to deal with this problem and consequently the Synod of the Church, as the Synod Report later records, received 'a remit from the Northern Presbytery, craving a ruling of the Synod as to the position of Mr John Murray, M.A., M.Th., divinity student.' The Report continues:

> The Rev. N. Cameron, after referring to Mr Murray's attitude towards the Synod's resolution on the Sabbath-travelling question and his action in going to Princeton Seminary, a seminary which had been abandoned by certain orthodox teachers on grounds of conscience, without the consent of his Presbytery, moved as follows: 'That the Synod give Mr John Murray till 30th October, 1930, to consider seriously his attitude, as in opposition both to the Northern Presbytery, in his having gone to assist in Princeton Seminary without their sanction, and also to the Synod on the question of travelling by hired conveyances to Church on Sabbath, and if he will not withdraw from this opposition by that date he will no longer be considered as a student of this Church.'

Beyond question, the real 'offence' to the Synod lay in Murray's known support for William Matheson, and when the official word of the Synod's decision at length arrived in September 1930 he knew that the door at home was closed. No one felt it more deeply than his father who, in the following letter of August 1930, wrote in characteristic spirit to John:

> We are always glad to see your letters, one always every week but one since you went there which keeps our minds always easy.
>
> I am very glad for the news of your last letters, how the Lord is leading you and how he has opened a door for you in his good providence. No doubt but it is the Lord that has done it and in all that came round these last years. The Lord was working in his wise providence to bring about his own purposes.

Of course, the Church had an end in view in sending you to America; perhaps that may not be the end the Lord had in view at all. One thing was keeping my mind easy since a few years back and that was the Lord's Word, believing that he would fulfil it, but where I did not know. The Lord has a Church and a very small remnant here and there over all the world as well as in Scotland. Of course, in a way, I would wish you to be in Scotland, so that we might see you, but the Lord is wise, he is wisdom itself, and I ought to say, Thy will be done on earth as it is in heaven.

And now, if it is his blessed will to cast your lot there, may he be pleased in his Sovereign Grace to give you grace to seek his own Glory and the salvation of poor lost sinners in this world, and may he be pleased to give and keep strength of body and mind to you for your duty, which is not light—no wonder you should be concerned about it . . .

Hugh Ross' wife died. She was just after putting the supper on the table and fell dead at the end of the table and passed away. We are getting many a loud warning and are very hard and deaf to it . . . I am the only one now living of the family, and sure I need not expect to be left very long now in this world! May the ever blessed One have mercy on me! What an account I have to give for all the years and privileges I have got in this world . . . May the Blessed One be in you and about you!

Your loving father,
Alexr. Murray

John Murray had come to see the call to Westminster as a call which he could not refuse. But with characteristic reticence, and out of a dislike of adverse reflections upon other Christians, he says nothing of his denominational problems when the letter of acceptance was finally sent:

309 Alexander Hall,
Princeton, N.J.
15th Sept. 1930

My Dear Dr Machen,

I owe a reply to your very kind letter of June 25th. I was always delaying an answer until I should be able to say that I officially accept the position of Instructor in Westminster Seminary. I did not have the decision of my Presbytery until a few days ago and consequently it is only now that I am announcing my acceptance of the appointment by the Board of Trustees. Though keenly aware of my great limitations, and insufficiency for the performance of the task, nevertheless I do with great pleasure accept, and I hope and pray with you that I shall find Westminster Seminary to offer the best field of service. I do trust that we shall experience much of the blessedness that springs from unity in the truth and that we shall be enabled in untrammelled and concerted action to further the Kingdom which is righteousness and peace and joy in the Holy Spirit.

In hope of seeing you very soon and with very warmest regards,

I remain,
Very Sincerely Yours,
John Murray

It is apparent that Murray would have been welcome to remain at Princeton. With his usual courtesy he had paid a visit to the home of J. Ross Stevenson before leaving the Seminary later in that same month of September. The President was out when he called, but wrote a few days later:

By Paths Not Known

It was most gracious of you to call at our house to say 'Goodbye', and I am exceedingly sorry that I was not at home at the time. We appreciate the faithful service you have rendered to your Alma Mater and deeply regret that you could not see your way clear to continue with us. Our best wishes follow you.

4

Alongside Gresham Machen

STANDING TODAY[1] before the rather gloomy four-storied house which is 1528 Pine Street, close to the centre of down-town Philadelphia, one finds it hard to imagine that in the 1930s it was vibrant with the life of youth. Built of brown stone, joined to the properties on either side in 'row house' or terrace fashion, and with the front door opening almost immediately on to the street, it was originally a rather superior nineteenth-century family residence. With the urban decay of the 1920s its desirability for that purpose had already declined, and the then owner, Oswald T. Allis, generously offered it as a location for the new Seminary to which he had already committed himself.

It was an offer which the Westminster Board of Trustees readily accepted. A team of carpenters prepared classrooms, the dining room was turned into a library, and less vital space was given to such things as the student eating club (beneath the old dining-room) and to offices. For staff it really required nothing more than a secretary and a married janitor, chiefly to be remembered for the 'normally acceptable' regularity with which he rang the electric bell for the opening and closing of classes. 'It was done in faithfulness to an old gold pocket-watch like that carried by a conductor on passenger trains in those times', as Paul Woolley remembered.[2]

---

[1] This account was first published in 1981.

[2] *The Significance of J. Gresham Machen Today*, 1977, p. 27.

For the next seven years, from September 1930 when the Seminary began the second year of its life, this was to be the centre of John Murray's life and work. Perhaps, as he reached his thirty-second birthday on 14 October 1930, he reflected on this, his first experience of living downtown in an American city. Gone were the open spaces to which he was accustomed, both in Scotland and at Princeton and, instead of rooms in historic Alexander Hall, his sleeping quarters were now at the very ordinary and inexpensive Gladstone Hotel, the upper floors of which were rented by the Seminary for student accommodation. The Gladstone was situated about ten minutes walk from the Seminary on the north-west corner of Eleventh Street and Pine Street, in an area which, says Woolley, supplied 'a good display of the seamier side of life'. 'A busy city with commercial elements, club houses, hotels, church towers, crumbling brownstone fronts and all the varied manifestations of urban life were there in contrast to the green trees and lawns of the Seminary campus in Princeton.'

Yet the location did nothing to dampen the enthusiasm with which Murray entered upon the work at 1528 Pine Street. He was back with senior teachers whom he had long esteemed. Back, also, with younger men who had been student contemporaries at Princeton and who were now also members of the Westminster Faculty. They were: Paul Woolley (Registrar, and Church History); Ned Stonehouse (assisting Machen in New Testament); Cornelius Van Til (Apologetics); and Allan A. MacRae (Old Testament). Unlike Princeton, the student body was now united in the belief of evangelical doctrine, and the whole Seminary was fired by a common commitment to a great cause. Faculty members readily gave of their substance to establish the new work: O. T. Allis, for example, asked for a mere peppercorn rent (one dollar a year) on his Pine Street property! 'For the cause of Westminster', writes William White, 'Machen was willing to pledge his life, his fortune, and his reputation.' One of the best illustrations of the spirit which united the men occurs in a letter from Machen to the President of the Student Association in 1931. He wrote from Baltimore, following the funeral of his mother, to thank the student body for the beautiful flowers and the expressions of sympathy which they had sent:

When I sat at the service yesterday afternoon in the old home where I was born, it was the thought of the comrades in Westminster Seminary which gave the most comfort, and to these comrades not only the Faculty but also the students belong. I think that is the most wonderful thing about our little company. Somehow I cannot think of myself as a 'teacher' in the midst of 'students' when I am with Westminster men; rather do we seem to be, above all, brethren and learners together as we study God's Word . . . God give us all, during the years of the Seminary course, and throughout all our lives, an ever-deepening fellowship with one another in Christ![1]

With leadership of this kind, the Westminster student body rose to the challenge of the unusual location. The sights they sometimes saw as they walked between the Seminary and their accommodation became an incentive to remember what lay before them as pastors. They felt, as Murray was to exhort a later generation of men to remember, that they were indeed preparing themselves 'in pursuance of a divine call for the ministry of that Word without which the whole world perishes in sin, in misery and death'.

Speaking of Murray's own contribution to this circle of men, William White has recorded in his biography of Van Til, 'Murray brought to Philadelphia a delightful Scottish burr in his speech, a rare insight into Scripture, and a devotional life that had a telling

[1] *J. Gresham Machen*, pp. 467–8.

impact on the lives of his students.'[1] More fully, his contemporary and colleague, Allan MacRae, writes:

> After Princeton, my next contact with John Murray was during the seven years when both of us were members of the Faculty of the new Westminster Theological Seminary. We were drawn to each other by our mutual commitment to the Reformed Faith and our solid determination to make the Word of God central in every aspect of life. An incidental factor that also contributed was the fact that except for Dr Machen, the head of the institution, we were the only members of the Faculty who were not married at that time. Consequently we had our main meal together at least three or four times a week and often took long walks in the country. Never in my life have I been associated with anyone with whom I found it more pleasant to discuss all manner of subjects. John had many interesting ideas and could express them with great clarity and insight. He also had the ability to lead one to dig into his own inner thoughts and find there ideas that he had not previously realized he possessed.

John differed from the other members of the Westminster Faculty on a number of what seemed to them to be secondary points. He never wavered in his practice, but rarely expressed himself on these matters except when he felt it necessary to do so. Sometimes this led to rather amusing situations. Thus once when Dr Machen and others, including Mr Murray, were at the home of Dr and Mrs Allis for Sunday dinner, the conversation turned to baseball. Dr Machen and others expressed their ideas about various players and about baseball games they had seen. Then Dr Allis' sister, observing that Mr Murray had taken no part in the conversation, graciously turned to him and said, 'Mr Murray, what is your opinion?' He replied, 'I never discuss baseball on the Sabbath.'

[19] *Van Til, Defender of the Faith* (New York: Thomas Nelson, 1979), p. 101.

One day John showed me a booklet entitled, *May Sabbath-Keeping Prevent Church-Going?* and told me that the author, who was a good friend of his, had been expelled from his Church because, though strongly opposed to ordinary use of any public means of transportation on the Sabbath, he had insisted that one should not be condemned for using public transportation as a means of getting to a church service. John evidently admired the spirit of his friend, and agreed with his principle. John himself, when invited to preach at a town a few miles from Philadelphia, would go on Saturday and return on Monday, spending two nights there, rather than spend twenty minutes travelling each way on the Sabbath.

John and I were often entertained at the home of a minister a few miles from the Seminary. The home included two little boys, both of whom have now become learned professors in American universities. One day we found the hostess greatly perturbed. She said that her dog had found a bottle of pills on which the stopper had not been tightly fastened, had managed to open it, had eaten all the pills, and an hour later had died. John's immediate response was, 'How fortunate that it was the dog and not one of the children!'

Since John and I were the two younger single members of the Faculty we were often entertained together at the homes of various other Faculty members. Subjects of conversation varied according to the interests of the faculty where we were visiting, and I always enjoyed seeing the activities of John's mind as he looked at many subjects from interesting viewpoints differing somewhat from those of us who had spent our youth on a different continent from that of his childhood.

One year John decided to spend the summer getting some acquaintance with the German language and German customs. Since I myself had previously spent two years studying at the University of Berlin, I was already adept in the German language, and on this particular summer I was planning to attend courses in Old Testament and Archaeology at the University of Berlin. It was my privilege that summer to explain to John the German customs where they differed from those familiar to him, and to act as interpreter for him on many occasions. After his experience of the bitter fighting in the First World War he often commented on the contrast between the attitudes of those years and the pleasant relations that we had with the German people, sometimes remarking: 'How strange life is; one day you are fighting a man, doing your best to kill him, and the next day you sleep in the same bed!

John Murray's decision to add German to his learning in the early thirties was typical of the determination with which he devoted himself to study. Princeton had given him a vision of what it meant to be a systematic theologian and he knew that he was still only on the threshold of the hard study necessary to that end. There was no short road to success, for a teacher of Systematic Theology must *first* be both an exegete of the Word of God and a biblical theologian. This was one main reason why, although J. Ross Stevenson, in the letter already quoted, had addressed his farewell greetings to 'Professor John Murray', he was to decline to receive that title until he was in his thirty-ninth year.

Murray's relation to Gresham Machen was basic during this period of his life and he came to aid Westminster's leader with ever increasing degrees of closeness. Machen's home was now a three-roomed apartment on the twenty-second floor of Chancellor-Hall, at 212 Thirteenth Street. He enjoyed that site partly because it was near the railway station, for railways (along with mountain climbing and football) were a favourite hobby, besides being his chief means of transport. Woolley well remembers Machen's routine. His day generally began with writing, then, with the morning's mail stuffed in the left-hand pocket of his overcoat, a hasty walk took him to Pine Street in time for the mid-morning chapel service. On some days, if his writing especially detained him, he might be twenty minutes later, in time for his first class at eleven o'clock. At lunch, frequently taken at the Drake Hotel, there were discussions with colleagues and thereafter he made his way to the part-time secretary, with whose help he handled his correspondence. At her office his left-hand pocket was emptied, after which, if a letter which he had answered was still needed, 'he stuffed it into the right-hand pocket of the overcoat next to a volume of the Loeb Classical Library. He always carried a Loeb volume with him to read in spare moments that were not available for other uses.'

In part, it was the increasing volume of Machen's correspondence in the 1930s which drew John Murray closer to him. Correspondents, ranging from missionaries to old ladies concerned at the number of murderers in their area, constantly wrote to Machen for advice. Questions received from ministers could be especially exacting if they were to be answered properly. By 1934, Machen was regularly looking for help from Murray's pen. Could he reply on his behalf to a communication from Dr Frank E. Gaebelein, he asks in a letter to John on 5 December 1934, and adds, 'I know that you are far more competent in this matter than I am.' On 12 December 1934, he wants Murray to answer an enquiry on reading material from Mr L. E. Froom of the Ministerial Association of Seventh-day Adventists: 'I wonder whether you could tell him anything and suggest anything to him to read. If you could, it seems to me that it would be a good piece of Christian service on your part. You are the world's best answerer of such inquiries and I am under a terrific pressure and strain just now.'

Similar letters with requests from Machen (all neatly typed) were to follow. One of Machen's ministerial correspondents wants advice on British Israelism, another needs a reading list on a given subject, while a third wants to know whether Calvinism is not the same as fatalism? This third enquiry Machen puts to Murray in the following terms:

May 6, 1935

Dear John,

I have received the following question:

'How would you explain the difference between the expression "What will be will be" and *Calvinism* or Predestination? The former is Fatalism, is it not? This question has troubled me. So many Presbyterians use the former term.'

It is an imposition upon you, but I am overworked beyond all possible endurance, and I wonder whether you would think it worth while to send this brother some kind of answer. He is Rev. W. W. Thompson, 53 Lawson Avenue, Claymont, Delaware. He was at Princeton in 1926, perhaps before your time. I have ventured to tell him that I am presenting his question to you. Do not trouble to answer it if it is too much of an imposition, but if you would send him just some little kind of reply, I should be mighty grateful.

You have certainly done fine service to many people in answering questions like this. I do not know anyone who can answer, and does answer, such questions better than you do. It is a burden, but I do believe that good is done by it sometimes.

Cordially yours, etc.

From the correspondence which survives between the two men it is clear that by the mid-thirties Murray had become Machen's closest adviser on questions of theology. In January 1935 the Seminary had extended its work by the start of a weekly radio programme entitled, 'Westminster Seminary Hour'. On these programmes, for part of the next two years, Machen was to preach the Reformed Faith. Behind the great simplicity and clarity of his utterance there sometimes lay much discussion on specific areas of doctrine and in this John Murray was especially involved. One morning in March 1935, for example, Machen rang Murray to speak with him on the Nicene Fathers' view of the 'eternal generation of Christ'. On the same day, concerned lest some of his words 'may not have been accurately stated and might consequently be misunderstood', Murray promptly sat down to write a full five pages to Machen on the subject in question, a document which unconsciously suggested that on this theme the writer had the whole field of Historical Theology at his finger-tips!

At a lunch-time consultation at the Drake Hotel, the following November, the subject was free-agency. As the time available did not suffice, later in the afternoon Machen got through to John at the Gladstone Hotel to continue the discussion on the phone. Even that was not enough, as is apparent from a letter from John to Machen the following day. We give this letter in full as an example of the kind of discussion in which the two men shared. Both were thoroughly agreed that while the Word of God must be preached in popular terms, no care could be too great to secure accuracy in handling the truth:

Gladstone Hotel,
11th and Pine Streets,
Philadelphia.
Nov. 23rd 1935

Dear Dr Machen,

I hope you will forgive me for cutting short our telephone conversation yesterday afternoon. The reason was that I had to leave for an appointment at six o'clock.

It may be that on the question of free agency we may not have come to mutual understanding. Free agency, of course, must rest upon the essential distinction between God and us, and this essential distinction expresses itself in the difference between God's infinite knowledge and the finite knowledge which in the nature of the case belongs to us. Finite knowledge is an attribute of the finite and with that fact our free agency is indissolubly associated.

Furthermore, human free agency must always be treated on the background of the absolute foreordination of God. It is in other words within the sphere of the absolute predetermination of God that we exercise our freedom.

Nevertheless, I do believe that your statement that 'The consciousness of the power of contrary choice is necessary to freedom' cannot be maintained.

Man as fallen is the bond-servant of sin. He cannot choose the good and reject the evil. He is *non posse non peccare*.[1] Within this, the most important sphere of his relations to God and to men, he does not have the power of contrary choice, and any consciousness of the power of contrary choice would be illusion or self-deception. But he is a free agent, even when he is the bond-servant of sin, that is to say, a free agent in the Augustinian-Calvinistic sense of the term. To say, however, that his free agency depended upon his consciousness of the power of contrary choice would be to say that his free agency rested upon an illusion, on something contrary to fact.

Furthermore it is to be remembered that it is not only within the sphere of voluntary or volitional decision that free agency obtains. There is, of course, a sphere within which the unregenerate as well as the regenerate man has the power of contrary choice, in which his free agency comes to expression in volitional decisions. But the area of free agency is very much wider. It includes everything for which he may be justified or condemned. Naturally man is depraved, but in that depravity he is a free agent. Indeed depravity can have no meaning except within the sphere of free agency. But

---

[1] 'Not able not to sin.'

his depravity as immanent disposition does not proceed from a decision, from a volition in the exercise of which he was conscious of possessing the power of contrary choice. His depravity expresses itself in decisions, but it exists as a fact for which he is responsible and stands condemned apart from these voluntary decisions.

Again the regenerate man is holy at the centre of his moral and spiritual being. That holiness is within the sphere of freedom, but it does not proceed from or consist in a decision.

Consequently the consciousness of which you speak, not being in accordance with all the cases in which free agency is operative, cannot be of the essence of free agency. As I said, I may not be understanding your position, but as you state it, it appears to me to involve the Pelagian position that the power of contrary choice is of the essence of free agency.

Trusting you will bear with me in this rather lengthy letter, and with very cordial regards, I am, very sincerely yours,

John Murray

Machen began a letter to John, four days later, with gratitude for this memorandum, 'which I am certainly going to find very useful indeed'. 'When I see you I want to talk about the matter under discussion a little more. I do want to hasten to say, however, that I abhor the notion that power of contrary choice is essential to freedom. Perhaps further discussion might reveal a little better what the point is about which I am still not sure whether I agree with you.'

In the same letter Machen repeated thanks to Murray for deputizing for him earlier that month in South Carolina in response to a request from President Grier of Erskine College for an address on 'The Inspiration of the Bible'. In a letter to Machen, following Murray's visit, Grier spoke of the address as 'the best treatment of that subject that he had heard'.

If it should be wondered why two men, working in the same building, needed to resort to correspondence to the extent which the above letters indicate, the answer is partly that events in the Church at large were increasingly taking Machen away from Pine Street. As already indicated, Machen had not regarded the withdrawal from Princeton as a closure of the battle against liberalism in the Presbyterian Church; rather he conceived the continuation of the struggle within the denomination to be a main part of the role of the new Seminary.

One reason why Westminster had been located in Philadelphia was the existence there of strong support from a number of churches in that Presbytery. Machen and his colleagues meant to work and pray for a new generation of preachers to be raised up who would turn back the tide of unbelief which had entered both the Church and her overseas missionary agencies.

It was, in fact, in the area of Foreign Missions that the developing crisis took a new turn. By 1932 it was clear to many that liberal theology was already entrenched in various branches of the Church's missionary programme. Appealing for action, Machen introduced an overture on the subject in his own Presbytery of New Brunswick in 1933.

Simultaneously he published a work of one hundred and ten pages entitled, *Modernism and the Board of Foreign Missions of the Presbyterian Church in the U.S.A.* In reply, the Board, in the person of its Secretary, Dr Robert E. Speer, insisted that there were no modernist missionaries on the field. 'Evidently', as Paul Woolley notes, 'there were two different definitions of modernism in use.' When, in that same year (1933), the General Assembly heartily endorsed their Board of Foreign Missions, the conservatives responded with the introduction of an institution (intended to operate within the denomination) entitled, 'The Independent Board for Presbyterian Foreign Missions'.

One writer has described the action of the conservatives at this stage as 'the earnestness of despair',[1] but Wilbur M. Smith, a member of the new Independent Board, has written to the contrary. He notes that even in the first year of the Board's existence it had started the support of some eighteen missionaries or missionary candidates and had a balance of $30,000 in the bank. 'There was', Smith believed, 'a real movement of the Spirit of God in this enterprise. We realized it was succeeding beyond all expectations.'[2] Whether that was so or not, it was soon to be apparent that a course of action had begun which could not continue without a split in the Presbyterian Church. The General Assembly of 1934 ruled that the Independent Board must at once cease functioning within the Church and that all Presbyterian ministers and laymen officially connected with it must sever their relationship immediately. When Machen, along with others, refused this ruling, his Presbytery found him guilty, although their sentence of suspension was delayed by Machen's appeal to the higher courts (the Presbytery's action was eventually upheld by the General Assembly of 1936). Similar action was in hand against others.

Murray had left America, homeward-bound for a summer in Scotland, before the General Assembly of 1935 was over. From the *Duchess of Bedford* he commenced a letter to Machen on 4 June:

> This is just a greeting to you from the Atlantic. I do hope you are well and that you are none the worse of the tiring experience of having to endure the proceedings of the General Assembly. I left before full reports came to me, but I saw that Messrs. Griffiths, MacPherson and MacIntire were finally refused their seats in the Assembly. It only further illustrates the tyranny of those in control of the Presbyterian Church.

[1] L. Loetscher, *The Broadening Church* (Philadelphia: University of Pennsylvania Press, 1954), p. 148.   [2] Wilbur M. Smith, *Before I Forget*, 1971, p. 114.

Machen replied in a long letter to Badbea on 17 June which included the following:

It was exceedingly good of you to send me a word from the boat. I rejoice in knowing that you are well on your way to your home, much though I miss seeing you even during the comparatively brief summer months.

The Assembly was indeed utterly ruthless. No doubt you will receive the forthcoming number of *Christianity Today*, in which Griffiths' account of the Assembly will be given. I am making sure, by sending you an extra copy by first-class mail, that you receive the forthcoming number of *The Independent Board Bulletin*, for which I have written a little bit of an article . . .

I am inclined to think that matters are coming more and more to a head. The plan of Mark Matthews and others seems to be to have Synod condemn Brumbaugh and then proceed at once to oust the session of Brumbaugh's church and take charge of the property.[1] It is needless to say that this will be resisted by the congregation. I do hope that we are moving towards a real Presbyterian Church. There are many things that are still dark about the way in which that is to be done. We do not know what God may have in store for us in the next year or two.

I do trust that you may have a restful summer. It will be a joy to see you again when the term begins.

Cordially yours, etc.

Machen had rightly judged the action that was to be necessary if they were not to submit to the demands of the General

---

[1] The Rev. Roy Talmage Brumbaugh was pastor of the First Presbyterian Church of Tacoma, Washington, which declared itself to be an independent church in 1935. As with other churches which then and later left the denomination, the Presbyterian Church in the U.S.A. moved to seize the property, and almost always succeeded in doing so.

Assembly. He saw that it was not only the continuance of the Independent Board which was now threatened, for presbyteries had begun to question all candidates for licensing and ordination on their position in regard to this division, an action bound to hinder Westminster graduates from entering the Presbyterian ministry. Accordingly, later in June 1935, a group of conservatives identified with Westminster and the Independent Board pledged themselves in a 'Covenant Union' to make 'every effort to bring about a reform of the existing church organization' or, in the event of failure, to be 'ready to perpetuate the true Presbyterian Church in the U.S.A., regardless of cost'.

When Murray returned to Philadelphia in September 1935, to begin an academic year with a record number of sixty-eight students, it was to share with Machen in the most difficult winter of his leader's life. Problems now began to multiply simultaneously on several fronts. Some who supported Westminster had never favoured the Independent Board; others, and notably Dr Samuel Craig, had become members of the Board, but in the face of the hostile denominational action they now drew back, their attitude to the denomination amounting to a policy of 'stay in at all costs'. Craig, Editor of *Christianity Today*, turned against Machen, even, in January 1936, to the point of favouring the shutting down of Westminster Seminary. By that date a small majority of the Westminster Board of Trustees were against action to form another denomination and accordingly resigned, the most serious resignation of all being that of the Faculty Member, Dr O. T. Allis.[1] As Robert Dick Wilson had died in 1930, Machen was now the last of the senior Princeton professors who joined Westminster at its foundation. But, painful though these losses were to Machen, he

[1] Craig, in *Christianity Today*, February 1936, referred to 13 out of the 28 Westminster trustees as having resigned and, as one had 'already resigned and another says he will', this was, he claimed, a majority.

was to encounter still more distressing problems from the younger and inexperienced men who were prepared, with him, to defy the General Assembly. The fundamental question before them was no longer Modernism, but the nature of the new denomination which they envisaged. Would it be distinctly Reformed and Presbyterian, fully committed to the Puritan theology of the *Westminster Confession of Faith*, or more loosely 'fundamentalist' in belief and independent in its church polity?

In one form or another, that question was now at the centre of Machen's chief discussions with Murray and, next to Machen, Murray became the foremost spokesman for the need of a full-strength commitment to Reformed theology. Accordingly, when Machen founded a new monthly, *The Presbyterian Guardian,* in October 1935 (to replace the influence lost with *Christianity Today*), it was Murray who was asked to write a series of articles entitled, 'The Reformed Faith and Modern Substitutes'. The series began in the issue of December 1935 and ran successively until August of the following year. Hitherto Murray had only written very occasionally for publication. In the August 1931 issue of *The Homiletic Review*, for instance, he contributed an incisive article on the atonement, which the Editor had asked for to balance a liberal's treatment of the same theme.[1] But although Murray wrote comparatively little before 1935, his colleagues knew that the gift was there. In a letter to him, following upon their discussion on the Person of Christ and the doctrine of the Trinity, Machen had commented in March 1935: 'Every time I appeal to you for help, I am impressed anew, not only with your learning but with your power of expression.'

The series on 'The Reformed Faith and Modern Substitutes' fully confirmed Machen's confidence. The first of the seven articles

---

[1] *The Homiletic Review,* New York, August 1931, pp. 93–8.

was a terse and trenchant survey of the prevailing defection in the Presbyterian Church in the U.S.A. 'It is no exaggeration to say that the situation in the Presbyterian Church in the USA at the present time is unspeakably bad . . . The default in the sacred province of discipline has been colossal. In view of this the whole Church as an organization is involved in the guilt of tolerating the most baneful heresy, a guilt of which the orthodox themselves, we are sorry to say, are by no means free. We have a state of corruption beyond the power of words to estimate, and ruinous in its consequences . . .'

In the second article, Murray proceeded to argue that much more was needed than a negative opposition to Modernism. A renewed commitment to the Church's Confession of Faith was required, and such commitment could not exist without a recognition that good reasons lay behind the denominational distinctions within Protestantism: 'The Evangelical Methodist or Lutheran believes that the Bible is the Word of God, but neither accepts the Confession of Faith of the Presbyterian Church. Both reject very vital elements that belong to the very essence of the system of Doctrine it contains.' He continued: 'There are certain brands of thought and belief widely prevalent within the Protestant Churches which we have much reason to fear have made serious inroads upon the orthodoxy of many in the Presbyterian Churches. Two of these types of thought, because of their pervasiveness, call now for more special mention. They are "Arminianism" and "Modern Dispensationalism".'

Although he did not explicitly say so, Murray knew that these two errors were characteristic of the 'fundamentalism' which many Bible-believers in America had come to confuse with historic Christianity.[1] Men whose outlook was broadly 'fundamentalist'

---

[1] Murray's colleague, R. B. Kuiper, was explicit when, writing in the *Banner* in September 1936, he spoke of 'the two errors which are so extremely prevalent among American fundamentalists, Arminianism and the Dispensationalism of the Scofield Bible'.

were anti-liberal, pro-missions and pro-evangelism, but, by reason of their admixture of beliefs, incapable of a full-orbed endorsement of the Reformed Faith. In the articles which followed he proceeded to show why the doctrinal distinctions made in the Westminster Confession remained vitally important: they concerned issues closely related both to the glory of God and to the life and spirituality of the church:

> The denial of unconditional election strikes at the heart of the doctrine of the grace of God. The grace of God is absolutely sovereign, and every failure to recognize and appreciate the absolute sovereignty of God in His saving grace is an expression of the pride of the human heart. It rests upon the demand that God can deal differently with men in the matter of salvation only because they have made themselves to differ. In its ultimate elements it means that the determining factor in salvation is what man himself does, and that is just tantamount to saying that it is not God who determines the salvation of men, but men determine their own salvation; it is not God who saves, but man saves himself. This is precisely the issue.

On the difference between Arminian and Calvinistic doctrine in regard to the death of Christ he writes:

> Did Christ die and offer Himself a sacrifice to God to make the salvation of all men possible, or did He offer Himself a sacrifice to God to secure infallibly the salvation of His people? Arminians profess the former and deny the latter; our Standards, in accordance, as we believe, with Holy Scripture teach the latter . . . Let it not be thought that the Arminian by his doctrine escapes limited atonement. The truth is that he professes a despicable doctrine of limited atonement. He professes an atonement that is tragically limited in its efficacy and power, an atonement that does not

secure the salvation of any. He indeed eliminates from the atonement that which makes it supremely precious to the Christian heart. In B. B. Warfield's words, 'The substance of the atonement is evaporated, that it may be given a universal reference.' What we mean is, that unless we resort to the position of universal restoration for all mankind—a position against which the witness of Scripture is decisive—an interpretation of the atonement in universal terms must nullify its properly substitutive and redemptive character. We must take our choice between a limited extent and a limited efficacy, or rather between a limited atonement and an atonement without efficacy. It either infallibly saves the elect or it actually saves none.

In subsequent articles he dealt with 'Modern Dispensationalism' in equally decisive terms. Dispensationalism, as revealed in the notes of the Scofield Bible, 'discovers in the several dispensations of God's redemptive revelation distinct and even contrary principles of divine procedure and thus destroys the unity of God's dealings with fallen mankind'. 'It is', he declared, 'heterodox from the standpoint of the Reformed Faith.'

Commenting on this controversy within a movement which was united in opposition to liberalism, some have argued that to polarize differences among evangelical Presbyterians, as these articles undoubtedly did, was singularly inopportune. It meant that attention was being turned from a common enemy to a policy which entailed criticism and divisions between brethren. 'First things', which had drawn so many together around Machen, were being thrust into second place by the needless debate which this policy was producing.

In the words of one supporter of this viewpoint, 'The great original purpose of the [Independent] Board to launch a movement supporting evangelical, truly orthodox missions, became secondary.'[1] Similarly, Craig complained that as a tactician Machen 'is about the world's worst'.[2] No doubt Murray was included in these criticisms.

But it can be shown that the policy being followed by Machen, and strongly supported by Murray, was not a deviation from an original higher purpose. Machen was the prime mover in both the Seminary and the Independent Board, and in his case it is misleading to say, as Wilbur Smith does, that the matters brought to the fore in 1935, 'were never in the minds of the originators of the Independent Board'. In a personal letter to Ned B. Stonehouse on February 25, 1928, Machen had written: 'I quite agree with you in holding that not some sickly interdenominationalism, or some kind of "fundamentalism" without roots in a scholarly past, but the Reformed Faith in its entirety, represents the hope for the future.'[3] Similarly, in his first address on 'Westminster Theological Seminary: Its Place and Purpose', in 1929, Machen had warned of the danger that, in the interests of a wider unity with other evangelicals, the Seminary might moderate its full commitment to the doctrine which had been foundational to the old Princeton:

> We rejoice in the approximations to that body of truth which other systems of theology contain; we rejoice in our Christian fellowship with other evangelical churches; we hope that members of other churches, despite our Calvinism, may be willing to enter into Westminster Seminary as students and to listen to what we may have to say. But we cannot consent to impoverish our message by setting forth less than what we find the Scriptures to contain; and we believe that we shall best serve our fellow-Christians, from whatever church they may come, if we set forth, not some vague greatest

[1] Wilbur Smith, *Before I Forget*, p. 121.
[2] Words used by Craig in the February 1936 issue of *Christianity Today*.
[3] MS. letter in Machen papers.

common measure among various creeds, but that great historic Faith that has come through Augustine and Calvin to our own Presbyterian Church. Glorious is the heritage of the Reformed Faith. God grant that it may go forth to new triumphs even in the present time of unbelief![1]

The *real* explanation for the tensions which, by 1935, had developed within the movement around the Seminary and the Independent Board of Foreign Missions was, in the words of Stonehouse, that hitherto 'the difference between the Reformed Faith and current fundamentalism [had] failed to come to full disclosure and understanding'.[2] Machen was prepared to face that 'disclosure' because he was concerned with long-term principles and not with mere 'tactics'. 'A true Reformation', he had written in 1925, 'would be characterized by just what is missing in the Modernism of the present day; it would be characterized above all by an heroic honesty which for the sake of principle would push all consideration of consequences aside.'[3]

The year 1936 was bringing differences to a head because, as the formation of a new denomination became inescapable for those who could not go back, the doctrinal commitment which that denomination would adopt had to be determined. This was the background to the Murray articles on 'The Reformed Faith and Modern Substitutes', and even before the series was finished, an assembly of the Covenant Union, meeting in Philadelphia on 11 June 1936, took the decisive step of forming 'the Presbyterian Church of America'. Subsequently, after protest and legal action from the denomination from which they withdrew, the name was changed to the Orthodox Presbyterian Church. With Machen as Moderator, thirty-four ministers

---

[1] *What Is Christianity?*, 1951, p. 229.
[2] *J. Gresham Machen, p.* 458.
[3] *What Is Faith?*, p. 103.

and seventeen ruling elders signed a declaration stating their purpose, and their decision to associate together, along 'with all Christian people who do and will adhere to us'. By November the number of ministers had risen to 106.

Before the historic meeting of 11 June, Machen was apprehensive concerning the confessional statement to which office-bearers of the new denomination would be required to subscribe. Although Murray's church membership was still with the Free Presbyterian Church, he was closely involved in the thought which had already been given privately to this issue. In March 1935, as part of the wider discussion, he had provided Machen with material (eleven typed pages) on 'The Decline of Creed Subscription in the Presbyterian Churches in Scotland'. Before the critical meetings of the Covenant Union in June 1936 it was known that some of the younger men, led by Carl McIntire and J. Oliver Buswell, Jr, favoured the view that the *Westminster Confession* should be subscribed to, *along with* amendments passed by the Presbyterian Church in 1903 which had been introduced, as many thought, to qualify and water down the doctrine of the Confession with respect to Calvinism. When June came, John Murray was away preaching in Canada, and on 6 June Machen telegrammed for his return as follows:

> It is extremely important that you should be present here on at least the first day of the Covenant Union meetings June eleventh and it would be well if you could be present also on the following day. Your counsel might also be valuable on Wednesday, June tenth. It seems likely that serious opposition will arise against elimination of nineteen hundred and three amendments to Confession of Faith. Your help is greatly needed.

Murray replied immediately, 'Anxious to do everything within my power for the continuing Presbyterian Church', but, in view of his commitments in Canada, he asked Machen to inform him of any developments which might make his journey unnecessary.

In the event, he did not travel, perhaps because of an agreement in Philadelphia that the disputed question of the amendments be postponed. The subject, however, continued to be debated, and the *Presbyterian Guardian* for September 1936 included another significant article from Murray's pen entitled 'Shall We Include the Revision of 1903 in Our Creed?' On this same issue Machen had also solicited the help of his old friend Caspar Wistar Hodge. Hodge, despite his continuance at Princeton, remained close to Machen, even to the extent of sending financial aid to Westminster and to the Independent Board. In particular, Machen wanted Hodge's opinion on B. B. Warfield's evaluation of the significance of the 1903 version, for Warfield had issued a pamphlet of 39 pages on the subject in 1904.[1] Warfield's critique of the revision had been mild, a fact which now made it possible for some to plead his authority against the call of Machen and Murray that the amendments should be dropped entirely.

A letter from Hodge to Machen, respecting the Warfield pamphlet, on 22 September 1936, includes a tribute to his former assistant in its opening paragraph:

Dear Das:

I was glad to see you once more. Classes are coming on me and I am so old that I have to prepare for each one, as I did not use to do. But I have spent the morning studying the additions to the Revised Confession and the article by B. B. Warfield. John Murray knows more about it than I do, but I will offer a few remarks—the result of my hasty study!

---

[1] It is reprinted in *Selected Shorter Writings of Benjamin B. Warfield*, ed. J. E. Meeter, vol. 2, 1973, pp. 370–410.

Hodge's letter went on to make some valuable doctrinal observations, but Hodge was not able to commit himself to a decision:
'As to whether or not the Confession as revised is self-contradic-
tory or whether it destroys the Reformed system of doctrine, I am
unprepared to say . . .' The elderly Princeton professor concludes,
'My time is largely spent in somewhat heated defense of you.'

Just two days later, Hodge wrote to Machen again, for since his
previous letter he had read John Murray's article in the pages of the
Guardian, referred to above. The difference of opinion between
Warfield and Murray as to the significance of the 1903 revision and
amendments deeply interested Hodge, and while he is not decisively swayed by Murray's article, it is clear that he viewed the
thirty-eight-year-old Scot as fully competent to express disagreement with one of Princeton's greatest teachers:

> I can't help feeling that Dr Warfield's article was too apologetic
> altogether, but I think it exceedingly plausible, and were he alive
> and arguing with John Murray, whose fine article in the Guardian
> I have just read, I imagine B.B.W. would unearth authorities to get
> the better of John. However that may be, what Murray says about
> the purpose of creed making at the time of the Westminster Con-
> fession and that of ecclesiastics of modern days, has my approval
> and admiration of the way he has said it. Also I agree with his state-
> ments about infant salvation, though B.B.W. followed Chas.
> Hodge and wrote at length to prove that the best Refd. thought in
> America and elsewhere was on his side.

Although the new denomination was launched without division
in June 1936 a separation of sympathies was already apparent. A
number of the younger men, led by McIntire and Buswell, began
to voice increasing objections as they were confronted with a
choice between the Reformed Faith and the fundamentalism with
which they had much in common. Before the end of the year

Machen faced the greatest blow of his life, when these men, who had earlier so gladly followed his counsel, proposed another leader to replace him as President of the Board of Independent Foreign Missions. 'Machen', writes Woolley, 'fully realized how seriously this situation threatened the Independent Board.' If the Buswell-McIntire forces were victorious, it was probable that the Independent Board would adopt policies that would impair, at the best, and annul, at the worst, its Reformed character. By a very close margin Machen lost the election. Further, at the Second General Assembly of the Presbyterian Church of America,[1] in November 1936, Buswell was appointed Moderator. In the words of an anonymous observer, Machen had 'the shock of recognizing that his ideal was not being realized, even among the small fragment of the doctrinally true Presbyterians'.[2]

The one thing that kept Machen from being broken-hearted was the conviction that it was always better to stand for principles, over against any short-term benefit to be gained from expediency. In the midst of almost overwhelming demands upon him, Machen pressed on with his work as usual, teaching, preaching, corresponding and organizing. Another book appeared from his pen, *The Christian Faith in the Modern World*, made up of some of his recently-broadcast addresses, delivered under the auspices of Westminster Theological Seminary. In a preface he wrote of his indebtedness 'to colleagues in the Faculty of the Seminary, particularly to Mr John Murray, who is in charge of the Department of Systematic Theology, for counsel generously given with regard to certain of the subjects treated in the lectures.'

---

[1] As noted above, this was the name adopted for the new denomination until 1939, when it was changed to the Orthodox Presbyterian Church. This followed a law suit brought against it by the Presbyterian Church in the U.S.A.

[2] Wilbur Smith, *op. cit.*, p. 119.

In December 1936 the subject upon which Machen and John Murray spoke deeply together, in one of their customary discussions, was 'the active obedience of Christ'; that is to say, the truth that Christ not only paid for the guilt of the sins of his people but, by his perfect obedience to all the precepts of the law, places his righteousness to their account. In the words of Murray, 'So by the grace of God complete remission of sin and of its penalty is grounded in real satisfaction to law and justice.'

On 23 December 1936, Machen sent Murray a further request for help. It concerned a correspondent whose letter 'makes my head swim'. Then, during the brief Christmas vacation, despite a cold, Machen went off to preach for struggling young churches in North Dakota. Before the New Year he was in hospital suffering from pneumonia. To a ministerial friend who called to see him on New Year's Eve he spoke of a vision he had had of being in heaven, adding, 'Sam, it was glorious, it was glorious.' The following day he was largely unconscious, but at one point his mind was clear enough to dictate a final telegram. It was sent to John Murray and read, 'I'm so thankful for active obedience of Christ. No hope without it.'

The next word which Murray received was that Machen had died at 7.30 p.m. on that same day, 1 January 1937. He was fifty-five.

There was much in Gresham Machen that John Murray was never to forget. In him he witnessed the extent to which hostility and persecution may sometimes go against a faithful witness. He also saw the grace which may keep a man from allowing anything 'to mar or compromise his supreme loyalty to Christ'. 'Of Bunyan's characters', Murray said, in a tribute written twenty-eight years after his death, 'Dr Machen was Valiant-for-Truth.'[1]

---

[1] From his Foreword to the first British edition of Machen's *The Christian View of Man* (London: Banner of Truth, 1965).

That element did not pass with Machen's death, and in the days ahead Murray was often heard to use such words as these:

> Expediency is not the rule that guides Westminster Seminary. It would sometimes be to our apparent advantage to suppress the testimony to certain aspects of truth, to soft-pedal on matters which wake the dissent and even provoke the ire of many people. Many things for which we stand are unpopular and we lose friends. Sometimes we are tempted to stand for things which the counsel of God does not warrant and we could gain a great deal of popular support by standing for them. We cannot do it, for we must not go farther than the counsel of God. The whole counsel of God but nothing more. The counsel of God and nothing less.

5

The Struggles of the Later Thirties

I N THE MID-1930S it was still by no means clear to John Murray
that his life's work lay in the on-going ministry of Westminster
Seminary. For one thing, the continuance of the Seminary, with no
property of its own, and almost constantly buffeted by controversy,
was itself unsure. In October 1935 he had come, with Machen and
the majority of the Faculty, to agree to resignation as the only
alternative, if the trustees insisted on a policy of conciliation with
the Presbyterian Church. Instead, as we have seen, there were res-
ignations from the board of trustees and O. T. Allis's departure
from the Faculty. The change of leadership in the Independent
Board of Foreign Missions in 1936 meant that henceforth that
institution was to be lost to definite Reformed convictions, and as
the dawn of 1937 brought Machen's death, inevitably there were
doubts over both the Seminary and the future of the Orthodox
Presbyterian Church. Paul Woolley, commenting on the possibility that, if Machen's pneumonia had occurred a few years later, he
might have been treated with penicillin and other antibiotics,
nevertheless goes on: 'But God does everything well. The immediately succeeding years would have produced much greater anguish
of heart than Machen had yet suffered. We would like to know
how he would have met the varied problems, but God took him
from the suffering that would have ensued and exchanged it for
His presence. We can be grateful through our tears.'

For both the young denomination and the Seminary the particular doctrinal issues in controversy among those who had left the Presbyterian Church were clear by 1937. As already observed, a considerable segment of men were hostile to the criticism of dispensational prophetic principles. Despite what Murray had written to the contrary, they were unable to admit that premillennialism could be distinguished from dispensationalism, perhaps because, in several cases, the two things overlapped in their personal creeds. Dr Allan MacRae, Professor of Old Testament at Westminster and premillennial in his personal convictions, complained that 'strong pressure is brought to bear upon the students to give up this doctrine'. In the Chicago presbytery of the denomination, Wilbur Smith writes that differences over prophecy became so irreconcilable that a division ensued.

To some extent the question of independency in church government (the view that *all* denominational affiliation is necessarily wrong) had also entered the general debate, but a far more critical issue was the question whether living a 'surrendered life' demanded abstinence from alcoholic drinks. It was part of the *mores* of the fundamentalist ethos that such a repudiation was a required part of Christian holiness. John Murray led the opposition to this viewpoint within the Seminary and notes still survive which he had prepared for critical Faculty discussions on the issue early in 1937. Characteristically he was determined that it should be judged from Scripture: he was in no way opposed to the personal act of Christians in denying themselves the use of alcohol, nor was he ever complacent about the fearful abuse of liquor (such as he had seen during the First World War), but he was vehement in his assertion that for the church to demand abstinence, in the name of Christian holiness, was to set up a standard other than the Word of God. In other words, a broad, vital principle concerning the sufficiency of Scripture was at stake. As he later wrote in *The Presbyterian Guardian*:

The Struggles of the Later Thirties

Many evangelical Christians today seek to impose standards of conduct and criteria of holiness that have no warrant from Scripture and that even in some cases cut athwart Scripture principles, precepts and example. The adoption of extra-scriptural rules and regulations have sometimes been made to appear very necessary and even commendable. But we must not judge according to the appearance but judge righteous judgment. Such impositions are an attack upon the sufficiency of Scripture and the holiness of God, for they subtly imply that the standard of holiness God had given us in His Word is not adequate and needs to be supplemented by our additions and importations. When properly analyzed this attitude of mind is gravely wicked. It is an invasion upon our God-given liberty just because it is an invasion upon the sufficiency of the law of God, the perfect law of liberty. It is therefore, appearances to the contrary, a thoroughly antinomian frame of mind. It evinces a lamentable lack of jealousy for the perfection of Scripture and invariably, if not corrected and renounced, leads to an ethical looseness in the matter of express divine commands. In the words of Professor R. B. Kuiper, 'The man who today forbids what God allows, tomorrow will allow what God forbids.'[1]

Within the Westminster Faculty his friend Allan MacRae took an opposing view on abstinence, as well as on premillennialism. Matters came to a head in April 1937 with McRae's resignation, followed by that of Dr Harold S. Laird, who was secretary of the Board of Trustees. Before the General Assembly of the Orthodox Presbyterian Church met in June, members of the Independent Board of Foreign Missions who still supported a fuller Reformed commitment resigned from that organization, and when the Assembly convened it adopted a resolution urging the Church to give no further support to the Board. With the majority of the

[1] *The Presbyterian Guardian*, 10 May 1941.

87

denomination voting in this manner it was clear that the Seminary also had the support of the larger part of the Church. Overtures to the Assembly asking for the adoption of total abstinence were defeated, and accordingly a strong-minded minority, led by fourteen ministers, withdrew to form 'the Bible Presbyterian Church' with their own Seminary. At their first Synod they were to alter the *Westminster Confession* so that it would express the premillennial view.[1]

Other men, originally in the movement which had begun the founding of Westminster Seminary in 1929, were also to drop out in various directions, and thus forces which had at one time apparently been so united were sadly weakened and divided. In Wilbur Smith's view, 'What began as a powerful thrust for the evangelical faith, a repudiation of modernism and inclusiveness, dwindled to minor proportions.' But, as already noted, John Murray saw it differently. The trouble was a basic lack of homogeneity among the men who had separated, a commitment, in too many cases, to the *Westminster Confession* without a sure understanding of what that *Confession* contained. Back in 1921, when Machen had spoken to the dying Warfield of his 'hope that to end the present intolerable condition there might be a great split in the Church', the latter had replied, 'No, you can't split rotten wood.' The troubles of the 1930s had only brought, in Stonehouse's phrase, to 'full disclosure' how far Presbyterianism had gone from its original strength and vision.

The Faculty at Westminster were under no illusions concerning the long uphill road which lay ahead in the summer of 1937. In the years 1937–8 the numbers in the student body fell from forty to twenty-eight. Not until 1953 were they to pass the fifty mark again. One effect of the crisis through which the Orthodox Presbyterian Church had to pass was to bring the Westminster Faculty to close

---

[1] Edwin H. Rian, *The Presbyterian Conflict* (Eerdmans, 1940), p. 243.

their ranks as ministers in the young denomination. Cornelius Van Til and R. B. Kuiper thus transferred their ministerial affiliation from the Christian Reformed Church, a Calvinistic denomination largely composed of immigrants from the Netherlands, and John Murray also decided where his church responsibility now lay. Nearly ten years later than he had originally expected, he was ordained to the work of the ministry by the Orthodox Presbyterian Church Presbytery of New York and New England on 28 May 1937, in Calvin Presbyterian Church, New Haven, Connecticut, the sermon being preached by Van Til.

The reason why Murray was ordained in Connecticut rather than in the Presbytery of Philadelphia requires explanation as it reveals an important feature of his life. Along with the other members of Westminster's first Faculty, while he saw the necessity of defending the faith, that was not the main purpose for which men were to be prepared: the positive spreading of the gospel and the proclamation of the whole counsel of God was the chief end in view. If John Murray had been left to his own preference it would have led him to the pastorate and the constant care of souls which is involved in the ministry of the Word. Love for people was a primary quality in his life. As it was, he sought to combine the training of students with such opportunities for outreach as were afforded to him, especially in the long vacations from May to September. He looked forward to these months, and when they came he gave himself as eagerly to people as he did to study in the winter. He warned his students against the idea that studies were the end of the gospel ministry:

> You must not forget that you exercise this ministry upon earth, in the ministry of the gospel to saved and unsaved men and women who also live in this world with its cares and concerns, joys and sorrows, miseries and disappointments. You must never think that

you are a spiritual aristocrat beneath whose dignity and office it is to minister, it may be, in the squalor of the lowest strata of society and in the midst of the discouragements of the lowest grades of intellectual capacity.

It was because of this emphasis in his life that in 1936, the year before he was ordained, he was appointed chairman of a newly-formed 'Committee for the Propagation of the Reformed Faith in New England'. Thereafter, in the words of Paul Woolley, 'He poured a considerable measure of his talents, time and resources into the rebirth of puritanism in New England through the establishment of Orthodox Presbyterian churches.' For about eleven weeks in the summer of 1936 Murray and eight others were to work in New England, covering much ground both by car and bicycle and linking preaching with house visitation. Writing on the need of New England in *The Presbyterian Guardian* in the spring of 1937, he expressed the hope that as many as fifteen men might be sent the next summer:

> We wish we had sufficient funds and men so that we could send a hundred. Even then we should only be touching the fringe of the need in this greatly unevangelized field. A great door and effectual is opened unto us. We pray for consecration in ourselves. We pray for the same in the men who will be sent, and for the baptism of the Spirit upon them. May they in true apostolic fashion turn that world upside down!

By the blessing of God the work of this Committee bore fruit in the formation of congregations, and Paul Woolley commented on how there were, at the time he wrote, eight Orthodox Presbyterian churches and one chapel in the State of Maine (the north-eastern extension of Massachusetts Bay Colony in Puritan days), where there was originally only one in 1936. John Murray's attachment to New England explains why he was ordained in Connecticut and why, though living in Pennsylvania, he became a life-long member of his denomination's New York and New England Presbytery.

It was in view of his known experience, as well as of his knowledge of the Word of God, that he was, during the first decade of the Orthodox Presbyterian Church's life, appointed Secretary of the Committee of Local Evangelism. His influence in that Committee is to be seen in the six reports which were drawn up relative to that subject, and sent out under his name to all ministers and sessions of the Church. In one of these reports on 'The Open-Air Meeting', after statements on the biblical basis and on contemporary problems respecting such meetings, the following rules are set down and expanded:

1. Go where the people are, not where you hope they will come . . .

2. Go in absolute confidence in the truth and power of the Gospel and in complete reliance upon the Holy Spirit to bless. Only as the love of God is shed abroad in our hearts by the Holy Spirit can we proclaim boldly, convincingly, and winsomely the everlasting gospel. To this end, we need to pray that we might be filled with the Spirit. Nothing can draw and hold so well and so surely in an open-air service as the preaching of the Word in the power of the Spirit.

3. There are successful ways of gathering a good audience. One way is to have a nucleus of Christians to go with the minister . . . A method that has been used by some Roman Catholics with real success in drawing a crowd is the question and answer method . . .

These reports give the best kind of directions in evangelism, and it is a loss to the church that they have been buried in obscurity while much inferior material has received prominence![1]

[1] They were discussed at the Tenth and Eleventh General Assemblies. It might be added at this point that when John Murray undertook his many sea

The progress in New England was undoubtedly an encouragement in the year that followed Machen's death and so, also, to a lesser extent, was the removal of the Seminary to a permanent site in Chestnut Hill, in the outer suburbs of Philadelphia. On what had been the Harrison estate, the Seminary obtained spacious grounds, a large house (renamed Machen Hall), a roomy stable-block which was converted into a library, two gatehouses, and a smaller frame residence. Besides supplying offices, classrooms and dining hall, Machen Hall was to be large enough to provide sleeping quarters for students for many years to come, and Murray (the only bachelor on the Faculty) took up his residence in a large room on the second floor. A number of years later he was to move to the two rooms on the top (third) floor which thereafter became known as 'Murray Heights'. But he did not wholly welcome this removal of the Seminary to its new location in the fall of 1937. At Chestnut Hill he was virtually in the countryside and he certainly enjoyed all the variety of bird, animal, and plant life with which the estate then abounded. Yet he missed the conveniences of 'Center City' Philadelphia and, in that respect, preferred the original location.

It was at this same period, after the formation of the Orthodox Presbyterian Church, that Murray became committed to one congregation in Philadelphia. Prior to 1936 he most frequently attended the ministry of his Princeton classmate, David Freeman, who was then minister of Grace Presbyterian Church, not far from Pine Street. It was the Freeman family who provided the welcome hospitality already referred to by Allan MacRae. Of Freeman's preaching Murray wrote in later years: 'I well remember the joy of

voyages between the USA and Britain, usually on one of the 'Queens' of the Cunard Line, he would obtain permission to put up a notice announcing that he would be conducting Bible studies in a room which was allocated to him for that purpose.

listening to the faithful and impassioned delivery of the gospel message from the pulpit of Grace Presbyterian Church.' He was by no means a critic of preachers, but one thing he did require was that a man *felt* what he preached: 'To me preaching without passion is not preaching at all.' It was the presence of this qualification which also led him in his early years in Philadelphia to be present occasionally at the church of a certain black preacher: 'He would say some excellent things. Of course, there were some things I could not agree with, but I can take Methodism from a Methodist!'

When, after the division of 1936, Mr Freeman became minister of New Covenant Orthodox Presbyterian Church, and, later, after an interval of a few years, of Knox Presbyterian Church, John Murray gave his full commitment. For the next twenty-five years he was to regard Freeman as his pastor.

In the 19th century, when Dr John Duncan attended upon the ministry of A. Moody Stuart in Edinburgh, the latter used to comment on how the worship seemed to be enriched. This was also Dr Freeman's experience with respect to the presence of his friend in the congregation: 'He appropriated the worship as his own, as though there was no one else in the place. God was before his mind and eyes. He was *intent* upon hearing the Word read and preached. I never saw anyone enjoying the singing of praise as he did.'

On those occasions when John Murray preached, Dr Freeman also recalls, 'His whole countenance, his whole being, was taken up.' But this stirring of emotion was also to be seen in him as a member of the congregation, and on one occasion, as a communicant at the Lord's Supper, his feelings simply overflowed.

In later years, Calvin Freeman, one of the two sons of the Freeman home, was to write:

For some reason I like to feel that I knew Mr Murray better than anyone else. This of course could not be true, but there is a sense in which it might be. I literally grew up with Mr Murray and cannot remember a time when he was not a regular 'guest' in our home. As far as memories go back, that is how far my memories of Mr Murray go. While I do not remember this, he must have squeezed and kissed me as a baby in the same way that I remember him doing the same to countless other children.

It is not really fair to speak of Mr Murray as a guest; he was really a member of our family. Each Lord's Day, for as long as I can remember, he attended my father's church and then came home with us to spend the day. And then we would go again to church at night and often he would have a snack with us after church. As a rule, during the week, he would be around at least once for dinner. The usual procedure after dinner was for him to send me to the store for ice-cream. This was quite an occasion in those days. He would take a crisp dollar bill from his wallet, put it in my hand and emphatically direct me to the store to buy a quart of ice-cream. It was part of his manner to seem very strict even in an act of obvious kindness.

I used to watch Mr Murray on the Sabbath. He would get his Bible, and hold it out open in front of his face as he leaned back on his chair; I never got the impression that he was reading. He seemed rather to be focused on one particular passage or verse. He would sometimes compare it with his Greek Testament and then focus back on the King James. His ability to meditate in the quiet of our home seemed to be interminable, for we children were taught to respect Mr Murray's preference for Sabbath quietude.

That is not all he did on the Sabbath. After dinner my brother and I got a long lesson. Mr Murray would teach us for at least an hour, sometimes two, and then we were allowed out for our walk. It is funny, the things I remember. One thing I shall never forget relates to when he was talking about Jacob's death [*Gen.* 49:33]. 'And when Jacob had made an end of commanding his sons, *he gathered up his feet into the bed,* and yielded up the ghost and was gathered unto his people.' I can hear him stressing the point of Jacob's composure; quiet, confident and with apparent strong assurance he gathers up his feet into his bed and dies. It was just as if he were lying down for a night's sleep. Nothing more! I can hear Mr Murray say those very words just as clearly as if he were with me now. I often thought since, that with the same kind of composure Mr Murray himself would die.

Strange how I would also remember his talking about the word *Mesopotamia* in connection with Abraham. 'I don't believe there is another word that has the same sound and beauty', he would say. He said the word again and again. Also the word *magnanimous* he liked and once explained its meaning. I believe it was in connection with Abraham's character.

The memory verses I learned from Mr Murray each week were well chosen. I did not realize at the time that many of them were the Messianic Prophecies. I understood, of course, the Messianic nature of Isaiah 53, but I did not understand that he was taking me through a sampling of progressive revelation when he started with Genesis 3:15, '. . . it shall bruise thy head. . .' and then to Genesis 9:25–27 '. . . Blessed be the Lord God of Shem . . . God shall enlarge Japheth . . . and he shall dwell in the tents of Shem . . .'; and then Genesis 12:1–3, 'I will bless them that bless thee and curse him that curseth thee; and in thee shall all families of the earth be blessed.' Each prophecy elaborates a little more on the line from which victory over Satan would come. Nor did I realize that he was drilling into me the necessity of faith when we learned Genesis 15:1–6 and the episode of Abraham's test in Genesis 22. These words linger in my mind to this day, and I remain indebted to him for having compelled me to learn them.

Mr Murray's teaching on Sabbath afternoons, his life, his presence, left an indelible mark on my life. Even some of his mannerisms and ways I have unconsciously adopted. I was teased about this by his family in Scotland many years later when I visited there. The need for being meticulous, for being concerned about the minutest 'details', even the prepositions of Scripture became a part of my whole way of life, a part of me, largely because of Mr Murray's drilling me so carefully in my formative years. As much by his example as by his words, he impressed upon me a true reverence and respect for Scripture. Mr Murray really believed that the Bible was the Word of God—no question about that—and you could sense it in his every breath.

Other personal memories of John Murray at this period come from the pen of Lawrence R. Eyres who was a student at Westminster from 1935 to 1938. Eyres writes:

I think I commenced a more-than-student-teacher relationship with him at the end of my first year at Westminster. I served that summer under the Committee for the Propagation of the Reformed Faith in New England. This was made up of John Murray, together with David Freeman, John H. Skilton and William P. Green. It was my field to labour in two or three small communities outside Portland, Maine. One of these was the village of Gorham, Maine. I commenced a Friday evening Bible study in the home of Mr and Mrs William A. MacDonald. Mr Murray was visiting with me at the very first of these classes (if my memory serves me right). Besides study, we began with a period of informal worship. I had a stack of old, dilapidated Gospel song-books from which we sang. Now I knew Mr Murray's views on inspired psalmody. We were not singing paraphrases at the time. Nor were we doing bravely at our singing. So I was not prepared for the shock of hearing Mr Murray join us in singing with evident fervour these uninspired hymns. Most of them were not worthy of the old Presbyterian Hymnal then current. It certainly helped in our informal worship. I never summoned the courage to ask him how he could do that. It has since come to me that (1) he saw we were not making out very well in our singing, and (2) we were not then engaged in formal worship, hence, there was no reason of conscience for not pitching in and assisting us in our weak efforts. I have loved him for this ever since, because, though a man of highest principle, he understood those who differed from him and could on occasion identify with them. He was firm, but not unbending.

On the lighter side, I well remember worshipping with him on a Lord's Day morning, somewhere around that same time, in the Second Parish Presbyterian Church in Portland, Maine (of which John Skilton was still pastor). During the service something happened to set off a baby in the congregation who continued to cry long and loud. In speaking with him afterward, I suggested that maybe it was the singing of the choir that started the baby off. With a twinkle in his eye Mr Murray said, 'No, Lawrence, I think it was the organ.'

In connection with our mutual involvement in the Committee for the Propagation of the Reformed Faith in New England, it was impressed on me that though Mr Murray was frugal by disposition (how could he be anything else?), he was not 'Scotch' in the usual sense of that word. I have no sure way of knowing, though I suspect that a major share of the funds that went into the financing of the Committee came out of his generous stewardship. I recall how, in the spring of 1937, I was asked to select three very much used automobiles for use among the summer workers under the committee that summer (I being one of them). I ran down, with a little help, three old cars at the combined cost of $150. One of these for sure, and I suspect all of them, were purchased with checks drawn on his own account. He also paid for licenses and, for one, a 'new' set of used tyres.

I became closer still to Mr Murray at the beginning of my senior year when, in the fall of 1937, the Seminary was moved to its present campus near Glenside, Pennsylvania. Mr Murray was faced with a problem. He could not in conscience, ride in public conveyances on the Sabbath. But neither could he now walk to his customary place of worship. An automobile was necessary. He first learned that he was eligible for a driver's license in Pennsylvania, despite the loss of his right eye. He then bought a fairly good used car at an automobile auction. But he couldn't drive. That year I regularly supplied the pulpit of a very small Orthodox Presbyterian congregation in south Philadelphia, not far from the New Covenant Church pastored by David Freeman where he regularly worshipped. Dr Freeman and I have the distinction of teaching him to drive. It wasn't easy. A couple of times we were nearly struck attempting to cross a through highway. It was difficult for him to master the art of 'clutching' and shifting while he scanned 180 degrees of traffic with his one eye. However, we must have been able teachers or have had an apt pupil, because he became a good driver. I never heard of his having an accident. But that year he hadn't yet mastered inner city driving. So, on Lord's Day mornings, and Wednesday evenings, I'd drive him to the Freeman home at 720 Carpenter Lane in the Germanstown section of Philadelphia. From there I would go by public conveyance to my post in south Philadelphia, stay the day, and then return in the evening to the Carpenter Lane house, spend some time in fellowship with Mr Murray and the Freeman family, then drive his car back to Westminster campus. Those were blessed times of fellowship indeed.

I well remember one incident at the Freeman's home. We were discussing the innate sinfulness of the human heart. Mr Murray had been holding forth on the depth of human depravity. Mrs Freeman then turned to him and protested, 'But Mr Murray, we know that you are not as bad as that.' I suspect she was meaning to pay him a compliment and, further, may not have been altogether serious. At any rate, compliment or whatever, he fixed her with his good eye and said in his sternest tone, 'Mrs Freeman, if you knew what a cesspool of iniquity this vile heart of mine is, you would never say such a thing!' She was rebuked. There was no more said on that subject.

During that same school year we were driving on a Lord's Day evening from a service where I had preached in one of our churches in New Haven, Connecticut. He commented on one part of the sermon from which he said he had been blessed. He refrained from commenting on another part, on which, on looking back, he might have levelled just criticism. He was too kind for that. Later on I asked him what he had paid for the car he had purchased. He had a short reply: 'I never discuss such things on the Sabbath.' This time I was rebuked.

I was married early in the summer of 1938. My wife and I first lived in a sparsely furnished manse in the little village of Deerfield, New Hampshire. Later that summer (and on subsequent occasions) Mr Murray was a guest in our home. He was a most gracious guest. I remember his telling my wife that, during my student days, if he could have got his hands on her he'd have shaken her. That in reference to my occasional absences from classes when I took off by Greyhound bus to visit her in her home in West Paris, Maine. My visits were testimony to the old adage that 'the course of true love never runs smooth'. I remember one time when our much loved black cat had just caught and killed a bird. My wife was scolding him for being so 'naughty'. Mr Murray intervened in behalf of the cat. He said, 'Gerry, you must not scold the cat. He's only acting according to his nature.' Strange how practical systematic theology can be!

At a Bible conference in Maine during the summer of 1939, Mr Murray spoke on the subject of the Virgin Birth of Christ (as I remember). Later I spoke to him saying that I appreciated the sermon. He said 'Lawrence, that was not a sermon; it was a lecture.' I then asked him what, in his view, was the difference. What he said I don't remember having been taught in my homiletics classes, but I have remembered it with profit to the present time. He said that a sermon has development and climax, and it is characterized by a passion which is not to be found in a mere lecture (though Mr Murray, it seems to me, always lectured with passion).

* * * * *

Before the 1930s closed there was confirmation that the fears which Westminster's original Faculty had all shared on the changing theological direction at Princeton Seminary were justified. After the death of Casper Wistar Hodge in 1937, the neo-orthodox Dr Emil Brunner had become a Guest Professor at Princeton Seminary and was invited to accept appointment to the chair of Systematic Theology, made famous by Archibald Alexander, the Hodges and Warfield. Like Karl Barth, Brunner did not believe in the infallibility of the Bible, nor even in Scripture as a trustworthy record of history. In the event Brunner did not take the permanent appointment, choosing rather to return to Switzerland in 1939, but it was clear enough that the Seminary, now under the Presidency of John A. Mackay, intended to break with its historic spiritual tradition.

They were not to do so, however, in the name of neo-orthodoxy; rather the claim was to be that they were 'returning' to the position of the Reformers as distinct from the 'narrow' seventeenth-century Puritan theology with which, as they regretted, Princeton had been associated. In a letter to Samuel G. Craig, who was leading an ineffective protest against the changes at Princeton, Brunner wrote:

> I think it is no news that President Mackay whilst differing in some points from me has the intention of leading Princeton Seminary back to the real Reformation theology, the real Biblical theology of which Warfield's theology is a decided deviation.[1]

In a word, this meant that the new Princeton was to be the 'genuine' interpreter of John Calvin, a claim which Murray was to answer effectively in several subsequent articles and reviews.[2] One practical step to counter the waning biblical influence of Princeton was the decision taken at Westminster in 1938 to establish a Journal, which, like the old *Princeton Theological Review*, would be a repository of Reformed thought upon issues of enduring importance. Thus the *Westminster Theological Journal* was born. John Murray was one of the two founding editors; the other was Paul Woolley, who attributes more credit to his colleague than would have been acceptable to him:

> He was one of the two editors of the *Westminster Theological Journal* for the first fifteen years of its existence. In that capacity it was he who was the creative figure. He knew what articles needed

---

[1] *Christianity Today*, Spring 1939, pp. 102–4, quoted by Rian, *op. cit.* pp. 267–8. Although Craig had disagreed with Machen in 1936, he wrote in 1938 that, since Princeton Seminary's reorganization in 1929, 'a number of things happened that would seem to indicate that the founders of Westminster Seminary were not far wrong when they maintained that a new Seminary was needed'. At this same date the Rev. E. G. Homrighausen, whose Reformed commitment no one attempted to prove, was appointed Professor of Religious Education at Princeton Seminary.

[2] See, for example, his review of Edward A. Dowey's *The Knowledge of God in Calvin's Theology*, reprinted in *Collected Writings of John Murray*, vol. 3 (Edinburgh: Banner of Truth, 1982), pp. 377–82.

to be written and who were the best people to write them. He was concerned about the impact of the *Journal* and scrutinized its text with meticulous care. He was not above the ordinary task of reading proof. His principle was that no trouble was too great to undertake, if it promoted accuracy in the text and clarity in the thought.

As the 1930s approached their close, and the Seminary completed the first decade of its testimony, the general scene in the churches presented no cause for satisfaction. Murray's feelings at that juncture are summed up in these words:

> O how crushing is the shame that rests upon the church! Humiliating indeed is the reproach. But by God's grace and Christ's power how glorious our vocation and responsibility! . . . Westminster Seminary raised a banner for the whole counsel of God when concrete events had made it more than apparent that Reformed churches throughout the world had laid in the dust that same banner, defaced, soiled and tattered. When the enemy came in like a flood, God in His abundant mercy and sovereign providence raised up a standard against him . . .
>
> We who are closely associated with Westminster Seminary have to confess that we have come far short of our profession and aim. Indeed, when we think of our own sins and shortcomings, we are amazed that God in His displeasure has not wrenched this banner out of our hands and given it to others more worthy than we. We marvel that God has not removed His candlestick out of our midst.
>
> But surely the facts show that He has not done so. In His abundant mercy He has borne with our sins and faults. I don't think it is presumption to say, and to say it to God's praise, that the banner has not been folded up and laid in the dust. We have not raised it aloft as we should have done, we have not unfurled it as we should. But it has not been lowered or furled.

6

Events in the War Years

FEW THINGS gave John Murray more happiness during his long
years in the States than visits from fellow-Britishers, and of
such visits perhaps none was more memorable than that of Dr
John MacLeod, Principal of the Free Church of Scotland College,
Edinburgh, in April 1939. MacLeod, then aged sixty-seven,
represented all that was best in the theology and piety of the Scottish Highlands and there was no living theologian with whom
Murray's judgment was in fuller accord. The occasion of the visit
was a series of lectures which John MacLeod was to deliver on
'Scottish Theology'. These he prefaced with an expression of his
hope that the faith of the Reformed Churches would have, 'in days
of reviving', an ample vindication, and in glory and power surpass
'the best and brightest days of its past'. A published volume,[1]
definitive in its field, was one enduring result of MacLeod's visit
to Chestnut Hill; another consequence, born of his esteem for
Murray and the witness of Westminster, was the gift from his
personal library of well over a thousand rare volumes of Puritan
divinity, both English and Scottish, and of the Latin Reformed
theology of the Continent.

Two months after MacLeod's days at Westminster he was with
Murray again, as they both spoke at 'The First American Calvinistic Conference', which met at Paterson, New Jersey. The theme

[1] John MacLeod, *Scottish Theology*, 1943; repr. Edinburgh: Banner of Truth, 1974.

was 'The Sovereignty of God', and it fell to Professor Murray to give the first address. By the standards of the day the subject was hardly appropriate, for the World Fair was then meeting in New York and man's achievements in the 1930s were the common subject of conversation. Within months however, as nations toppled before German and Russian armies, and Europe was once again engulfed in war, others were to learn of the need to 'take refuge in the absolute sovereignty of the eternal God'. As Murray was to write a few years later: 'It is an inexpressible comfort in these days of upheaval and turmoil to know that all events, great and small, are embraced in God's sovereign providence. Present history is not moving towards chaos. It is moving in the grand drama of God's plan and purpose to the accomplishment of His holy designs and to the vindication of His glory.'

In the summer of 1939, before the outbreak of war, John Murray was once more home in Scotland. The parting with his family at Badbea before re-crossing the Atlantic must have been particularly hard. When he would next return was entirely unknown; certainly he was unlikely to see his aged father again, and the whole future of the homeland to which he was so ardently attached, was threatened by the shadow of German aggression. Johan, his sister, had now taken up their father's former role, and all family and local news went to John in regular letters. In the midst of such items of information as she knew her brother to be eager to receive, Johan expresses these thoughts on the world scene in a letter of 21 December 1939:

> The poor Finlanders! It is to be feared that their country will be like
> Poland unless a miracle happens.
> Our own navy is putting up a brave fight. We do hope that they will
> be very successful against such danger . . .
> We are drawing to the close of another year. Many a year has passed

and we are still in the land of mercy. O to be made wise, but the things of time seem to be our great concern. We wish you all manner of happiness, dear John, and may God bless your work for His great Name's sake.

With the subsequent entrance of the United States into the Second World War, and general conscription into the Armed Forces, the life at Westminster Seminary was soon affected and the developments anticipated in the late 1930s had to await the post-war years. At one point the number of students in attendance was to fall as low as twenty. But the relative quietness at Chestnut Hill was not without its advantages to John Murray, and a considerable amount of written work was done both for the *Westminster Theological Journal* and for other publications. In 1941 he contributed three articles to the monthly *Calvin Forum* in an extended debate with Dr Albertus Pieters on the question whether the Fourth Commandment is still part of the moral law, and in 1942 and 1943 *The Presbyterian Guardian* carried a series of articles from his pen on 'The Westminster Assembly'. It was probably at this same period, the tercentenary of the meeting of the Assembly in 1643, that he also prepared his extensive lectures on 'The Westminster Confession', which were subsequently taken by many students as an elective course.

Among published work of a more popular kind which he prepared during the war years were a memorable address on 'God and the War',[1] given at the Christian World Order Conference in Cincinnati in 1942, and a broadcast address in September 1944, entitled 'The Light of the World'.

One effect which the war had upon the Seminary was to restrict its role almost entirely to that set down in its constitution, namely, 'To provide an adequate supply and succession of able and

---

[1] Reprinted in *Collected Writings,* vol. 1, pp. 344-55.

faithful ministers of the New Testament'. Before the war, and more so after it, the Seminary offered its facilities to those who wished to study theology without necessarily knowing a call to the ministry, a practice which has not been without its dangers. But while the United States government was prepared to exempt future ministers of the gospel from military service, it gave no such liberty to those who merely sought to read theology, and consequently Westminster was reduced to those who were genuinely candidates for the ministry.

John Murray made telling use of this fact in welcoming the members of the incoming class in June 1944:

> Unless for some physical reason you are ineligible for military service I hope you have felt something of the urge to enlist in the services of your country in the present emergency. Indeed, I hope you have felt that urge in a very potent way. I hope you have found it very difficult to take advantage of the opportunities and privileges that are now being given you, when so many of your fellow countrymen have to face the hardship and peril of the field of battle, and face these perils and endure so many hardships for the protection of the many privileges that are now yours. If perchance you have not weighed these considerations, then I hardly think your decision to follow the course upon which you have embarked is worthy of your privilege and of the task that is ahead of you . . .
>
> Why then do we welcome you to Westminster? On the assumption that yours has been a painful decision. Why do we congratulate you? We do so for this reason. You have come here, we trust, because of divine compulsion. You believe that you have been called by God to prepare yourselves for the gospel ministry. You are under the compulsion of a divine call to the greatest vocation upon earth . . . [1]

[1] The whole of this address is printed in *Collected Writings*, vol. 1, pp. 104-6.

It is not often that students entering a Seminary are greeted with an address as solemn and direct as the one from which we have just quoted. Yet the professor who spoke in such tones soon came to be known by each incoming class for those human qualities and notable kindnesses which won the affection of succeeding generations. He wished to be a 'father' as well as a teacher to his students and, as the following letter to David Freeman shows, few men ever had a clearer view of what a father can be.

January 9, 1942

I have to give you the sad news that my father passed away last Wednesday. I had a cable from my brother that night. The news of his passing brings a peculiar feeling of sorrow, but I am also filled with a deep feeling of gratitude and joy. He was a dear and eminently worthy father, so faithful, so loving. It is an inexpressible privilege to believe that he is now with the Lord and Saviour whom he loved and served for so long. Every indication points in the direction that the work of saving grace was wrought in him at a very early age, and with unimpeachable integrity and perseverance he witnessed to the Lord to the ripe age of 90. His interest was lively and his faculties unimpaired, until, just a few weeks ago, his interest in things of this world seemed largely to disappear. In the last letter I had from my sister she told me that, for the two days preceding, he was in the 51st Psalm and repeated it again and again from the beginning to the end in Gaelic, his mother tongue, of course.

Though he was my father I may say that there were few men in the Highlands of Scotland whose life and memory were surrounded by such fragrance, and whose life of consistent godliness claimed such veneration and respect. To be his son is a great privilege but also a tremendous responsibility. I wish I could have been home to pay the last rites of respect and love. Today or tomorrow will be the day of the funeral and his body will be laid over the dust of my mother whose body was laid in the layer of ground eight-and-a-half years ago. I cannot but think of that layer of ground. It is precious to us. Even the body of the believer is precious to the Lord; it is still united to Christ. My father's body will be raised one day when, with a shout, with the voice of the archangel and the trump of God, he will be raised to the consummation of the blessedness he yearned for. Well do I remember, when he would be teaching the young regarding the resurrection, how he would look at his own hands in affirming the reality of the bodily resurrection.

Well, now I suppose I could write all night along these lines, for under God I owe to none what I owe to my father. To the glory of God I could go on almost endlessly, expatiating on his virtues and sterling qualities. But the most prominent thought I would convey is that of glory to God for His wonderful grace. This is a day of sorrow for me, but it is also one of thanksgiving, and therefore the tears of sorrow are mixed with unspeakable joy.

With warm regards,
I am,
Very cordially
John Murray

We have already mentioned John Murray's commitment to the work in New Covenant and Knox Orthodox Presbyterian churches in Philadelphia. One of his most pleasant duties throughout the years was to teach a Bible Class after the morning service. The entire congregation was generally present including children and young people. To those who know him only by his writings it might seem almost incredible that he could be a regular and successful teacher of children, but the fact that it was so cannot be denied. Part of the explanation lay in his attitude towards the younger generation, for in any group of people they were always given the most affectionate of welcomes. 'His pats and his squeezes', comments Paul Woolley, 'alternately delighted their recipients by their affection, and terrified them by their well-intended but painful vigour.' But the teaching he gave them was also so lucid and suited to their capacity that none was discouraged and, in addition, he favoured the Bible class with a privilege which he did not encourage at Westminster, namely, a question-and-answer method of instruction. Through the foresight of a grown-up there exist verbatim accounts of some of his lessons to the class in 1943 and 1944, when they were going through the Book of Genesis.

A brief extract from a lesson on the deception which Rebekah encouraged Jacob to practise, in order to obtain the blessing of Isaac intended for Esau, will illustrate how these classes were conducted. After repeating the story, and emphasizing that Rebekah was intent on securing the blessing for Jacob, Murray addressed a question to Bobby, 'Why was she so intent on securing the blessing for Jacob?' 'He was the oldest', the youth replied hopefully. 'No, Jacob wasn't the oldest. Do you know, Richard? Martha?' Securing no help from his class, John Murray proceeded to explain how Rebekah was influenced by the promise made to her at the birth of Jacob and Esau, 'The elder shall serve the younger.' At this point a rather difficult question was addressed to David Freeman himself. There followed a question to Bobby, which he was able to answer. 'Now, Bobby, do you think that Rebekah was guilty of any deception in this matter?'

'Sure, yes.'

'And should she have practised that deception?' 'No, I don't think so.'

'What do you think, Martha? Louise? Didn't she have a good reason in view?'

'Yes, she had a good end, but the end didn't justify the means.'

'That's the point! That's very good. Did you all get that point Martha made? Rebekah was very jealous for the divine purpose and promise, but she resorted to a wrong means, the means of deception.' At this stage in the lesson the teacher took up the interesting but difficult question whether deception is ever justified, and he defined deception as something that is 'calculated and intended to create in the mind of another person an impression contrary to fact'. 'Now, what about war? Camouflage, is that not deception? You put out a dummy gun, you surround it with a lot of dummy shells and give the impression to the enemy that this is a very important position, and it is not so. Don't you try to create an impression that is wholly incorrect?'

We cannot stop to relate how the Seminary Professor went on to discuss the ethical problems related to the sanctity of truth,[1] except to record how in the course of doing so he drew a distinction between concealment and deception:

> Concealment in some instances may be deception. Yes, if you conceal something from a person when that person has a right to know and ought to know, that is deception. Suppose children conceal something from their parents that they ought to know, they are deceiving their parents. But to conceal something from a person when that person has no right to know is not deception. Mrs Soder doesn't need to tell me how much money she has in the bank. That's none of my business to know, and it is no deception on her part that she doesn't tell me. I don't tell Mr Freeman what my personal estate is, even though he is my best friend. He has no right to know. It wouldn't be wrong to tell him, but I'm not under any obligation to tell him . . . And, of course, there are certain things that everyone not only may, but should conceal. There are depths of thought in

---

[1] The reader can pursue the subject further in his book *Principles of Conduct: Aspects of Biblical Ethics* (Eerdmans, 1957), chapter 6.

the human breast that no one ought to expose to another . . . There are certain things that I never expect to tell any human being. I confess them to God, I hope, but I don't expect ever to tell them to any human being – certain thoughts that I have, and certain temptations, and so forth. No! It would be entirely unedifying to expose them, but concealment is not deception . . .

With lessons like this young people were both interested and made to think. A few words from another lesson reveal John Murray's conviction on the importance of teaching theology to teenagers. He was speaking on this occasion (16 April 1944) of Jacob's God being also the God of his grandfather Abraham. Of course, as he reminded the class, when Jacob fled to Padan-aram, Abraham was dead, for Jacob was then around seventy years of age. 'And', he added, 'Jacob was a good long while in Padan-aram before he was married . . . So there's some hope for me!' But Jacob was around fifteen years old before his grandfather's death: 'He probably had become personally acquainted in his youth with the godliness of his grandfather. A boy of fifteen who is very observant will acquire a very vivid recollection of his grandfather if he is acquainted with him, and especially if he was with his grandfather towards the end of his days. My father died two years ago and his grandchildren were pretty close to him in his last few years. I am sure they will never forget his death-bed and his last days!'

This led the speaker, who had earlier quoted Genesis 35:29 ('Isaac died, and was gathered unto his people'), to go on to speak of heaven and the gathering that will take place there at the resurrection. As is liable to happen to all teachers of children, he received a rather off-putting answer from one of his class as he questioned them:

'You know, for those who get to heaven it must, of course, be a supreme joy to see whom, Nancy? What will be the supreme vision of heaven? Do you understand my question?'

'No!'

'If you go to heaven, you expect to go to heaven, you hope to go to heaven, well, when you go to heaven, whom do you want to see? Yes, with your physical eye, as it were. I am thinking of the resurrection when we will be raised from the dead, when we will go into the final state of glory. Whom do you want to see most of all with your physical eye?'

'My mother! — I don't understand.'

'Who will be the centre of interest in heaven?'

'God.'

'Who will be in heaven in the flesh? Which person of the Godhead? Don't you think of Christ? You see, Christ will have a body in heaven as well as you. He has a body today. Don't you see? God the Father doesn't have a body and God the Holy Spirit doesn't have a body. But the Son does have a body. Do you know the *Shorter Catechism*? Who is the only Redeemer of God's elect, Martha?'

'The only Redeemer of God's elect is the Lord Jesus Christ, who, being the eternal Son of God, became man, and so was and continueth to be God and man in two distinct natures and one person for ever.'

'Do you know the *Shorter Catechism* to the end, all through? Do you, Richard? Do you, Martha? You, Nancy? How old are you, Nancy?'

'Thirteen.'

'Now everyone of you children should know the *Shorter Catechism* from the beginning to the end without a mistake by this age. Now that's without joking at all. At the age of twelve you ought to know the *Shorter Catechism* from beginning to end without even making a mistake. You don't know what you are missing! Get down to learning it, if you haven't already learned it! It will not only give you the most perfect human compendium of Christian truth that there is in the whole world, but it will be the finest mental exercise, and it will lay a foundation in your mind and in your life for a hundred other things as well as for true religion. The mere mental discipline of learning it with exactness down to each preposition is one of the best disciplines that we know of in this world in the field of education. The primary reason is to learn it for the purpose of having in your mind a comprehensive compendium of Christian truth, but even apart from that there are a hundred by-products. It will be invaluable to you through your whole life, and not only in this life, but in the life which is to come.

'Now, this seems to be far removed from the subject, but you can see how far afield you can get in studying text by text the Scriptures. This isn't far removed from the subject at all. I started off with this text here at the end of chapter 35, and we began to talk about heaven; and what I said was, or what I was going to say was, that it will be a great joy when we go to heaven, if we get there, to meet Abraham, Isaac and Jacob. But Abraham, Isaac and Jacob will not be the centre of interest in heaven, great as they were. The centre of interest, as Nancy said, will be God; and so far as physical appearance is concerned, the great centre of interest will be Christ Himself, "The Lamb who is in the midst of the throne." Now when we read these Old Testament stories with respect to the deeds of Abraham, Isaac and Jacob, we should think of heaven because they are in heaven. And we all of us profess to be true believers in Christ; and if we profess to be true believers in Christ, we are professing to be heaven-bound, and therefore some day we are expecting to meet Abraham, Isaac and Jacob face to face!'

Another area of the life of Knox Church where John Murray's help was long to be remembered was the work he did in counselling and advising those with personal problems. David Freeman regarded his pastoral ability in this work as outstanding and attributed it to 'his deep insight into Scripture; he knew and saw where the application of Scripture would be appropriate.' Unlike that type of counselling which is little more than Christianized psychology, Murray leaned on Scripture and gave a scriptural basis for the directions which he offered. Commonly this was of great aid to those whom he counselled and this prompted many to turn to him. David Freeman recalls one case of a young married couple with serious difficulties, who had come to him with problems which he was unable to resolve. Finding that they had confidence in John Murray, he rang the Seminary to tell Murray of the urgency of their difficulties and to ask him if he could visit them. Although the hour was late and the couple lived on the other side of the city, Murray went at once, and Freeman subsequently attributed the fact that things worked out well to the wisdom of his friend's handling of the situation.

John Murray's interest in the young was by no means confined to the Seminary and the Sabbath School at Knox Church. The education of youth was an uppermost consideration in his thinking, and that for theological reasons. In an article on 'The Christian World Order', which he wrote in 1943, he asserted that while 'a Christian world order, in the purity and completeness of its conception, will not antedate that manifestation of power and glory when Christ will come again without sin unto salvation', nonetheless, 'the Christian revelation does not allow us to do anything less than to formulate and work towards a Christian world order in the life that we now live.' There is, he argued, a divine obligation to see that true religion embraces every department of life: 'Industry, agriculture, education, recreation.'[1]

It was, with respect to education, that in the same year, 1943, he shared prominently in the launching of a movement upon which he set great importance. Along with Edwin H. Rian and Robert S.

[1] The article is reprinted in *Collected Writings*, vol. 1, pp. 356-66.

Marsden, he invited a number of other brethren to an informal discussion on the subject of a Christian University. The date was 23 March and the venue the Robert Morris Hotel in Philadelphia. The eventual result was an Association, undenominational in character, pledged to 'the establishment of a university . . . founded upon the adhering to the Christian system of truth and way of life as set forth in the Reformed or Calvinistic standards . . .' Support grew and Murray enthusiastically gave of his time and counsel. He was one of the committee of four which drew up 'The Constitution of the Christian University Association of America', and, as usual in such cases, he probably had a principal part in the drafting. The document, which was published, was accepted at a meeting in Grand Rapids on 29 June 1944, when the Association was formally established. In October 1944 it became incorporated in the Commonwealth of Pennsylvania as a non-profit corporation. About the same time the Association acquired a famous estate, with the mansion of a former millionaire, on the edge of Philadelphia for a mere $200,000 and expectation grew that, given the right Faculty members, a powerful new impetus for historic Christianity would soon exist in the educational field.

This is not the place to trace how the movement at length failed before a university was ever opened. There were legal problems (on the relationship between the Association's Constitution and Pennsylvanian law) and difficulties both personal and theological. According to articles written by Ned B. Stonehouse in *The Presbyterian Guardian*, it appears that a basic problem was the question how Calvinism should be defined.[1] Some had entered the Association with a very different view from that understood by Murray

---

[1] These articles were published in a booklet in 1947 entitled, *Calvinism and the Christian University*, which is the source of the subsequent information given. I have gone beyond the time period of the War Years in tracing this movement to its end in 1947.

and the other founding members. 'It was to be plain', writes Stonehouse, commenting on the Association's origins, 'that the movement wished to stand squarely in the stream of historic Calvinism, with all of its supposed narrowness and with all of its actual breadth. A barren Calvinism and hyper-Calvinism, on the one hand, and a watered-down, inclusive, broadly tolerant or concessive Calvinism on the other, were to be avoided.'

Stonehouse cited Professors Haroutunian and Pauck of Chicago, liberal scholars of that time, as holding misconceptions which the proposed University should avoid. They were critics of the 'narrow' Calvinism, but professed to see Barthianism as a legitimate form of Calvinism ('Barth and Brunner stand firmly in the Calvinistic theological tradition') and Haroutunian alleged that Machen's theology (*i.e.* the theology of the old Princeton Seminary) was an innovation, rather than historic Calvinism.

The final factor in what was to be the collapse of the whole Christian-University endeavour was the totally unexpected return of one of the initiators, Edwin Rian, from Westminster to Princeton Seminary, where he rejoined the denomination he had left with Machen and became Assistant to the President. The demise of the Association was one of the greatest disappointments of Murray's life. It failed, not because its principles were wrong, but because, in the words of one of its supporters, Dr Clarence Bouma, true Calvinism had become 'a pretty thin trickle'.

* * * * *

As the Second World War drew near its end, an American Forces chaplain, the Rev. Van Pernis, who had been in Britain and enjoyed the hospitality of the London home of Dr Murdo Tallach (a friend of John Murray in student days at Glasgow), wrote to his former host in April 1945:

I have been to see our mutual friend, Dr John Murray at Philadelphia. He was very happy to learn I had visited you . . . He is more than anxious to visit his homeland, relatives and friends, but is too conscientious to ask for a special travel permit at this critical hour. I love him for his sincerity, even as his students love him for his efficiency, his devotedness to his task and his godliness. He adorns our Seminary.

Later that same year John Murray was able to revisit home after six years of absence. It must have been one of Badbea's happiest days!

* * * * *

Before this chapter closes, one other episode from the late 1940s deserves inclusion. In July 1949 Murray attended the Sixteenth General Assembly of the Orthodox Presbyterian Church, which met in Los Angeles. There Lawrence R. Eyres met him, and was never to forget how the scenery of the West Coast of America affected his friend. The occasion provided, in Eyres' words, 'an outstanding insight into Professor Murray's heart, not merely as a Christian or a theologian, but as a theologian-Christian'. Eyres continues:

> He made a comprehensive trip of it, travelling by train and bus, taking in first the Grand Canyon in Arizona before arriving in Los Angeles. To him all God's works invoked worship. The Grand Canyon was the 'grandest' work of nature he had ever seen. But then he spent a few days with some of our vacationing pastors in Yosemite National Park in the High Sierras of north-central California. The Sierras succeeded to the 'grandest scenery' he had ever seen. At the close of the Assembly my wife and I invited him to ride with us and our four-year-old daughter back to Portland, Oregon, where he could take a train to Seattle and a coastal steamer thence

to Vancouver, B.C., and take a scenic train ride via the Canadian Pacific through the Canadian Rockies and back to Toronto to spend the rest of the summer. He gladly accepted our invitation, and we set out on our 1100-mile journey by the coastal route which took us through the towering Redwood groves of northern California. These trees I had seen before. They mildly impressed me as nothing more than big trees—and is not everything bigger in California? But not John Murray! As soon as we approached the first of these groves he said, as only he could say, 'Lawrence, we've got to stop.' (He had a way of saying those words like I've never heard them, with his Highland brogue.) And stop we did. He got out of the car, cast his eye the whole length of those 350-foot trunks, slapped his knee, and said with deepest reverence, 'Isn't that grand!' ('Grand' also came out uniquely to my American ears.) This performance was repeated fully half a dozen times: 'Lawrence, we've got to stop . . . Isn't that grand!' And each time, as he spoke, I looked again at those big trees and began to see their grandeur for the first time. John Murray could see through his one eye more of God's glory in these, his works, than I had seen with my two eyes.

By way of postscript to the above, he later told me that the Canadian Rockies were the 'grandest' of all.

From that memorable visit to the West Coast, Murray returned to Philadelphia with a large, heavy 'slice' of petrified redwood in his suitcase which he subsequently carried home to Scotland. Years later he found that his sisters, lacking his appreciation, had broken and dumped the specimen. He reclaimed one piece which still adorns the Murray home.

Badbea.

Loch Migdale, looking east towards Badbea (the first house visible on the lower slopes of the hill a little left of the centre of the picture).

A Communion service at Migdale, Sutherland, c. 1880,
with members of the Murray family undoubtedly present.

Alexander and
Catherine Murray.

Bonar Bridge School, c. 1910. John Murray is on the top right-hand corner of the picture and next to him his life-long friend Norman Stewart.

*John Murray in his student days in the
early 1920's.*

*Alexander Hall, Princeton Theological
Seminary.*

*The view west from the entrance to Badbea; the Creich Free Church can be seen on
the top right.*

Westminster Seminary Faculty in 1938, the first year on the new campus. Rear: Young, Murray. Seated: Stonehouse, Van Til, Kuiper, Woolley.

...en Hall,
...minster Seminary,
...delphia.

John, in the 1940's.

Christina and Johan.

William, who farmed Badbea until his death in 1963.

The Westminster Faculty in 1947. Seated: Woolley, Van Til, Kuiper, Stonehouse, Murray. Standing: Skilton, Young and Kerr.

As chairman of the Library Committee, conferring with Arthur Kuschke, the Librarian.

The most familiar sight of all, both on the Westminster Campus and elsewhere — a snap in California in 1960.

At the Leicester Conference, c. 1965.

Commencement Day at Westminster. From left, Professors Woolley, Stonehouse, Young and Murray.

Presiding as Moderator at the General Assembly of the Orthodox Presbyterian Church in 1961.

At the last General Assembly at which John Murray was present, in 1966, a scroll was presented to him by his fellow-commissioners containing the following tribute:

You have been a warm friend and counsellor to us, one and all, giving individual counsel whenever we sought — always out of a rich wealth of knowledge and inspiring reverence for the written Word.

You have been a faithful presbyter, spending untold days in the service of our beloved church, both in its assembly services and as a member of many of its committees.

You have been a gracious reprover, a hearty encourager, and an un-bitter dissenter in our deliberations.

To many of us you have been a patient teacher and more, for you have taught us exactness in the study of Holy Scripture, and a deep reverence for its high doctrine.

We honour you in our hearts. We respect you for your scholarship and wisdom. We are grateful to our God for you, Professor Murray. But we are compelled to say more: we love you dearly, and it is with deep sorrow that it appears that we may not see your face or hear your voice in future assemblies. We pray God that He may lay His hand on you for a most useful and happy ministry during your retirement years in your native land. We 'thank God on every remembrance of you'.

Father and son, 1972

With the other trustees of the Banner of Truth Trust. Rear: Ian Barter, Jim Grier, John Gosden. Front: Iain Murray (and Mrs Iain Murray) and Ernest Reisinger. At the opening of the Grey House, Edinburgh, April, 1973, the new headquarters of the Trust. John Murray had left home by 5 a.m. in the morning to be present on this occasion and had to return home the same day.

John and Valerie Murray, with Logan and Anne-Margaret, 1972.

Looking west from Badbea in the evening, a view unchanged in seventy-six years.

The graveyard at Bonar Bridge and the old family grave.

IN
LOVING MEMORY
OF
ALEXANDER MURRAY
BADBEA
DIED JAN. 7, 1942 AGED 90.
CATHARINE LOGAN
HIS BELOVED WIFE
DIED JULY 1, 1933 AGED 78.
THEIR SONS
DONALD AND THOMAS
LOST IN ACTION 1914-18.
WILLIAM
DIED JAN. 21, 1963 AGED 68.
THEIR DAUGHTER
JOHAN
DIED DEC. 9, 1966 AGED 85.

"THE LAST ENEMY THAT SHALL BE
DESTROYED IS DEATH." I COR. 15. 26.

7

The Seminary Professor

FOR JOHN MURRAY, through thirty-seven years, the most important hours which he spent every week in term time, were those occupied either in his classes or in preparation for them. Yet in these pages it is impossible to reflect the centrality which the classroom had in his life. In the nature of the case, class lectures provide little of biographical interest and his class-room procedures remained virtually the same for successive generations of students. When Westminster graduates of the 1960s compared notes with their seniors of the 1930s, they might observe developments in some areas of their professor's thought, but the essential features of his role as a teacher remained patently the same.

Invariably punctual for the start of a class hour, Murray's method was to begin with prayer (which he always took himself), and then to occupy most, if not all, of the remaining time with what amounted to a dictation of his lecture. He expected his students to be able to retain and reproduce his train of thought and, as his arguments were always closely knit, the only way they could do this successfully was by taking him down almost *verbatim.* 'The thing I remember most about his lectures in all his classes was that one dared not miss a word', writes Lawrence Eyres. 'To get the gist of his lectures required that a student write like a house on fire, or he might miss an essential link in his teaching. There was no fat, but all meat.' The truth is that to take

Murray's lectures down with exactness required a considerable degree of proficiency. Knowledge of Greek and Hebrew was assumed, and so was a good English vocabulary, for students soon learned that their professor chose words very deliberately: he believed that accuracy in thought required precise, apposite language. Usually his only pause in a lecture was to write a particularly difficult word on the blackboard, but for some students this practice was not followed frequently enough and they floundered when required to write down some of Murray's favourite English words for the first time!

The Professor was undeterred by the fact that his teaching method was out-of-fashion. He had seen it used effectively at Princeton Seminary and he judged that it had two enduring merits. First, it was consistent with what Warfield called 'the dogmatic spirit'.[1] Students were in theological seminaries, primarily, to receive truth, not to discuss and debate it; still less to originate ideas of their own. Certainly independency of judgment had to be developed, but that was to be the process of years: the immediate need of a theological student is to learn and to grasp an authoritative presentation of historic Christianity.

Secondly, and in connection with the above, Murray held that the dictation method of teaching was itself an important learning device. Speaking of this, Dr Calvin D. Freeman says: 'Hearing the words and writing them down, he thought, were very important means of driving an idea into the mind. I never did completely agree with him on this point, but in retrospect I can see some wisdom in his method, and I must confess I can still hear his lectures ringing in my ears.'

In the hands of other men this manner of lecturing might indeed be tedious, but Murray did not merely read a manuscript.

[1] See for example *Selected Shorter Writings of B. B. Warfield*, vol. 2, p. 663.

Although he might have delivered the same material many times before, he always prepared himself afresh. He wanted his subject to master both his mind and his spirit and from his opening words of prayer students knew that the work before them was more than the exercise of a classroom. 'Fear of God dominated Professor Murray's classroom', recalls Walter J. Chantry. 'Each period began with prayer from the professor's lips which brought all into the presence of an awesome God. Each subject was handled in a dignified and solemn manner that conveyed deep reverence for the Almighty. Professor Murray breathed the attitude that all things in his lectures were holy and majestic. Not a study of the fear of God, but the professor's visible and audible manifestation of that fear, became a main lesson for his young disciples.' Lawrence Eyres, a student some twenty-five years before Chantry, makes a similar observation:

> His usual manner, after opening prayers (which by way of reverence took his class to the very throne of God, so filled were they with the language and thought forms of Scripture), was to begin to speak very softly. We had to strain to catch his words. But not for long. As he would warm into his lecture his voice would rise to the fervour of his material. Every word and sentence was freighted with the consciousness of divine truth. His students of that period had a humorous expression for the rise of power in his voice. Those were the days of the Big Ben alarm clocks. They were advertised as designed to awake one gently but firmly. The ad line was, 'First he whispers, then he shouts.' Mr Murray was likened to Big Ben, as to the tone of his classroom lectures.

In the organization and presentation of his lecture-material, John Murray's great and constant characteristic was his total reliance upon the Scriptures. As a text-book in Systematic Theology he employed Charles Hodge's three volumes, as Warfield had been content to do (differing, in this regard, from J. H. Thornwell, who used Calvin's *Institutes,* and R. L. Dabney who used Turretin), yet Hodge was never the starting point upon any subject. The starting point was always the text of Scripture. Only after a detailed exegesis of the relevant texts in the original languages would he proceed to show how their teaching combined to formulate a doctrine. This careful scrutiny of the text of Scripture was never hurried over, and if, sometimes, the examination of the biblical language seemed as 'dry as dust', he would tell his hearers 'to remember that we are dealing with gold dust!' 'Never', comments Chantry, 'would he discuss a doctrine philosophically or logically with mere allusion to "proof texts".' His great concern, writes Paul Woolley, was not to impose or force anything upon the Scriptures: 'Rather the Bible text was drawn upon to build up and develop the doctrine. Murray devoted great care to that development. Every word in his formulation counted, for it was an attempt to represent the Scripture with faithful accuracy.' Cornelius Van Til has written more fully on this same point:

> The most important thing to be said about John Murray is that he was, above all else, a great exegete of the Word of God. When I say this I mean he was an expert in the exegesis of the whole of Scripture, of the Old as well as of the New Testament. I can still see him in the Faculty room talking about a problem of Old Testament exegesis with Edward J. Young, the Professor of Old Testament. Dr Schilder once said of Dr Greydanus that he had crept through the New Testament. Well, Murray had crept through the Old as well as the New Testament. Only an expert, like Joe Young, could get his attention before the Faculty meeting proper began. When I had the appointment to the chair of Systematic Theology at Calvin Seminary after the retirement of Professor Louis Berkhof, John advised me against accepting it. To teach Systematics properly one must,

first of all, be a biblical exegete. After that, one must be a biblical theologian in the way Professor Geerhardus Vos had been a biblical theologian in his day. Systematic Theology must, first, grow out of and be the ripe fruitage of penetrating, linguistic exegesis. Then, secondly, it must be the result of gathering together what biblical theology has found. The 'system' of Systematic Theology must, therefore, always be amenable to a development that springs from continued study of the Scriptures.

The impact of Murray's lectures was the impact of the Word of God itself, and by example he demonstrated the need for life-long study of the Holy Scriptures. In the teaching of the truth, the authority of the Bible stood unique and alone. So much was this the case that Norman Shepherd recalls, 'We used to say that the only bibliography in his books was the Scripture index.' Of course, it was not true; Murray's reading was broad, and he knew how to use it when occasion demanded, but his jealousy for Scripture controlled both his material and his manner of teaching. However much a Seminary might, in some respects, resemble an academic institution, he believed passionately that there was an essential difference. Theological seminaries exist to prepare men to speak, 'not in words which man's wisdom teacheth, but which the Holy Ghost teacheth' (*1 Cor.* 2:13), and he exemplified the Pauline conviction that to confront men with Scripture is to meet with God. 'Professor Murray was one of the godliest men that I have ever known', writes Dr Morton H Smith. 'To be able to sit in his class-room and take notes on his lectures was itself a religious experience, since he himself approached the material with such a deep sense of devotion.' Walter J. Chantry has a similar recollection:

> Reverent, precise exegesis was our daily fare in Professor Murray's lectures. Thus he fed our souls with that which is sweeter than honey and the honey comb. And thus he *showed* his pupils how to

study theology and how to feed solid meat to their flocks. Some
students wished that Professor Murray would adopt more popular
methods of class instruction. But in his methodology were to be
found some of his greatest lessons: fear of God, faithfulness to the
Word, precision in the communication of truth. Often I left his lectures longing to be able to do something to make known the riches
of God's Word which I had just heard.

Murray did not favour the interruption of his lectures with
questions. Norman Shepherd, a student in the 1950s, could not
recall it happening more than four or five times in all Murray's
classes which he attended. By the 1960s, in other professors' classes
at Westminster, questions during lectures were commonplace, and
not every student could appreciate the difference when it came to
Systematic Theology. Geoffrey Thomas remembers a voluble
Marxist turned evangelical who, on starting at the Seminary, was
as ready to stop Professor Murray with questions as he was the
other professors in their lectures. 'When Professor Murray asked
him to stop asking any more questions until the class was over he
cried, "I've got as much right to be here and speak as you have."
Professor Murray thereupon closed his lecture file and left the
classroom. The student never interrupted again!'

Murray's resistance to questions during lectures was probably
based upon his concern to maintain the development of his subject
without any digression or irrelevance. Any intrusion into his order
of thought would have been a distraction to others as well as to
himself. And, in any case, he had learned to anticipate the important questions and was ready to deal with them in due course.
William McDowell remembers how, when a student asked an
irrelevant question, Murray would say, 'Mr —, that question is not
to the point now. I shall take up your question when we have come
to the right time.' Probably six weeks passed and the student had

forgotten his own question, when, in the midst of his lecture, the professor said, 'Now Mr —, in regard to your question, let me say as follows.'

Justifying Professor Murray's practice with respect to the absence of class discussion Shepherd writes:

> It was more appropriate and rewarding for us to listen, to absorb, and to meditate on what our teacher had to say; to be led rather than to lead. The lasting impact of these sessions testifies to the wisdom of his preferred pedagogical method. We came away from his classes satisfied.

Nevertheless, the fact is that John Murray was a master in the art of answering questions. Sometimes, if an enquiry was made at the close of the lecture, he would answer it at once, his characteristic pose at such moments being to stand with one hand half-lifted towards his face, staring intently at his tightly clenched fingers. Once that stance was adopted students knew that the process of meditation by which the answer would be delivered had begun! More often, however, as the McDowell anecdote already given reveals, he would keep a classroom questioner waiting for a day, or even for weeks, before he gave a reply. It was alien to his whole spiritual make-up to provide an instant response to a question to which he had hitherto given little thought. To state the truth always required care, and he wanted to be sure he was not advocating anything that lacked the sanction of Scripture. As Shepherd says, his delays and his aversion to 'instant exegesis' were an important part of his whole approach to instruction: 'Our teacher was reminding us "that every idle word that men shall speak, they shall give account thereof in the day of judgment" (*Matt.* 12:36).'

Often there were questions to which Murray could have given a ready and, to most minds, a sufficient reply, but he chose to take time to look at them more thoroughly, and his final response would often reveal a consideration for their difficulties which often took students by surprise. Once a point was raised he never seemed to forget it until he had followed it through to a definite conclusion. 'Sometimes', remembers Allan Harman, 'I would find him taking up a topic again which I had discussed with him a week or two before. Often I had carried the matter no further, but he would tell me the conclusion he had come to, and then would trace out the lines of thought which he had followed.' On one occasion, at the end of a class, a student asked whether there was a verse in the New Testament that taught that every Christian has a duty to witness for Christ. He was thanked for his question and a few days later was given an answer on a piece of paper containing nearly twenty New Testament references! Needless to say, that scrap of paper was to be treasured by the questioner.

Calvin Freeman is of the opinion that some students who perhaps heard Murray answer little in class, and who never asked him anything privately, did not know 'how beautifully and thoroughly he could answer questions'. He writes:

> The secret that some never learned was to ask the question and then wait. It took a while for him to warm up. He would begin slowly, thinking as he went, and if left uninterrupted would continue for half an hour to an hour, sometimes more. The answers were given with humility, with appreciation, often with a sense of indebtedness to you for having asked the question. He seemed to use your questions to stimulate his thinking and was appreciative for 'thinking about things he might not otherwise have considered'. At the time of the execution of the Rosenbergs for treason, I questioned him on the propriety of capital punishment in such a case. 'I'm glad you asked that question, Calvin. That's something I never really gave any thought to.'

I wish I could have taped some of his eloquent responses to my questions. Once, as I recall, he gave me a rather complete exposition of Romans 14 in response to a question on Christian liberty. He could wax eloquent on that subject, and he would also expound in that connection 1 Timothy 4. Regarding responsibilities in marriage, as noted in 1 Corinthians 7, and the Roman Catholic view of Mary's virginity, I remember his very words: 'If Mary remained a virgin, she was a wretch indeed.'

I cannot reproduce in exact form all that Mr Murray told me, but I can remember with vividness a question I asked concerning Psalm 139, verses 21 and 22: 'Do not I hate them, O Lord, that hate thee? and am not I grieved with those that rise up against thee? I hate them with perfect hatred: I count them my enemies.' I could not understand how it was that God could hate when he is also the God of love. The usual answer to that question is that God hates sin but loves the sinner. Mr Murray recoiled from that explanation by pointing out that the sin and sinner cannot be set apart, that the sin is itself an expression of the sinner [cf. *Matt.* 15:19, '. . . out of the heart proceed evil thoughts . . .']. Moreover the text clearly says 'I hate *them* . . .' Mr Murray was a great one for sticking to the text. He was not going to resolve the issue by changing the text to suit the explanation. What he said in essence was this: hatred and love in the Scriptural sense are not mutually exclusive ideas; it is possible both to love and to hate at the same time. As a matter of fact, hate in the biblical sense can actually flow out from love. It is because God loves that He can abhor and detest them for their rebellion. His 'hatred' carries with it the desire for the sinner's repentance. It is in the sense of detestation that God hates, not in the sense of desiring to destroy or take revenge. God loathes them for their rebellion, but at the same time loves them and wishes for their repentance. This fits in well with what we read in Ezekiel, chapter 33, verse 11; 'As I live, saith the Lord, I have no pleasure in the death of the wicked.' God detests *them* but takes no pleasure in their death. He pleads with them earnestly, 'Why will ye die, O house of Israel?'

* * * * *

Humour was a rare feature in John Murray's lecture room. Occasionally in a dry form it might appear in his answer to a question. Once, after he had announced a forthcoming final examination, a student had the boldness to ask whether it would include the historical survey which had been given at the beginning of the lectures. 'Certainly it might', replied the professor, 'that is part of the course.' When the student replied that in past examinations no questions had been set on that part of the course, Murray responded: 'That was because in those years I just did not happen to ask a question on that part'!

A humorous interruption to a lecture was so comparatively unknown as to be remembered if it occurred. Once, when ground excavations had commenced close to the Seminary boundary in the 1960s and an earth-moving vehicle, known as a Caterpillar, had moved into the operations, the deafening roar of this vehicle as it accelerated distracted the class. The lecturer ignored it, but when the noise recurred, even more loudly, he broke off with the question, 'What's that?' 'A Caterpillar', was the immediate reply of one student. 'A *caterpillar!*' exclaimed the astonished professor, whose knowledge of agricultural machinery did not seem to extend to this piece of modern equipment! Laughter was unsuppressible!

Professor Murray's abiding seriousness in teaching was the direct consequence of his view of what it means to handle holy things. The use of any part of Scripture for the purpose of amusement he regarded as a grave sin. On the other hand, if a spiritual truth had been clearly established, he could respond to the practical humour in kind. A memorable instance of this once occurred at a conference of ministers of the Christian Reformed Church, where Dr Clarence Bouma and Murray debated the merits of total abstinence from all alcoholic drinks. Bouma argued for total abstinence on the grounds that 'demon alcohol was claiming, not its hundreds, but its thousands'. Murray was ready to grant that total abstinence was a legitimate choice for a Christian to make,[1] but the moderate use of alcohol was equally legitimate. After this discussion, a would-be facetious Dutchman asked Murray whether, if he were right there and then offered a glass of wine or whisky, he would accept it. 'Yes', Murray replied, 'If it's good stuff.' 'The audience roared', reports Van Til, 'but John blinked nary an eye', his straight face disguising his own enjoyment of the retort which the humorous questioner had deserved.

Commenting on Murray's characteristic gravity in spiritual things, Geoffrey Thomas writes:

> Any irreverence in humour he deplored. Once, a list of rules was posted up on the seminary notice-board and after each rule some student had written in pencil various textual references from the Bible. Mr Murray, seeing this, showed his immediate displeasure, and without delay obtained an eraser from the Faculty library in order to rub out the offending references. 'There is a place for humour, but this is not the way.' On another occasion a student with an artistic touch drew a series of cartoons with a monk as the central character, making references to various incidents on the campus. Professor Murray was not amused and took the cartoons down. When Karl Barth came to lecture in Princeton in 1962 a number of students went across to hear him and one evening Professor Murray and Dr Van Til

---

[1] 'It may well be that, in some cases, the cost of sobriety is total abstinence. The words of our Lord apply. It is better to enter into life with one eye, than having two eyes to go into the hell of fire.' See 'The Weak and the Strong' in *Collected Writings*, vol. 4, pp. 142–157.

went over. There followed the meeting of the famous protagonists, Barth and Van Til. In the car, on the return journey, reference was made to the way in which Barth had sought, at some points, to amuse his audience. 'I did not laugh', Mr Murray commented tersely.

Professor Murray's daily programme differed comparatively little through the years. After breakfast in the students' dining club in Machen Hall, he was always ready for work by 8.20 a.m. and, where it was possible so to arrange the schedule, he preferred to begin classroom work with the first lecture hour of the day at that time. His students did not always share that preference, and Ed Clowney remembers how, over-sleeping on one occasion, his rest was broken by a message from the Professor of Systematic Theology, requiring his presence in the classroom! On average Murray generally gave two daily lectures, Monday to Friday. In addition to his regular work in Systematic Theology, students had the opportunity to take elective courses from him at various periods. These included the *Westminster Confession of Faith*, Sanctification, Old Testament Biblical Theology, Christian Ethics, the Person and Work of Christ, the Epistle to the Romans, and Covenant Theology.

Following the custom at Princeton Seminary, there was a mid-morning break for worship at Westminster led usually by one of the professors. When it was Murray's turn to take this service, there was the singing of a psalm, followed by a talk of five to six minutes which was pithy, to the point, and meeting the need of the students.

The diligence with which Murray customarily worked was proverbial. At times when he had no lectures and was deeply involved in the preparation of written work, he could well spend the greater part of the day, until between nine to ten at night, working in his room, allowing himself only short interruptions for meals and to walk his regular 'Murray Mile' in the afternoon.

Whatever the weather he did not miss this exercise. Dr Van Til recalls one occasion when he had joined Murray and they encountered heavy rain. 'Neither of us had an umbrella. A woman stopped her car and said: "Can I give you gentlemen a ride?" "No, we are just out for a walk." "Oh", said the astounded lady, "Could any one be so foolish as to walk needlessly in the rain?"' In addition to this, he would often undertake some vigorous manual work around the Seminary grounds, shovelling snow in winter or sweeping up the abundance of fallen leaves in the autumn. His love for the open-air never left him, and in so far as he had other relaxations, it was in such things as watching the skunks playing on the lawn outside Machen Hall in the evening.

Once his writing on the *Romans* Commentary began in the 1950s he required a large number of books at hand, and his venue for daily work switched from his own quarters to a large table set aside for him in the old library. For years he was to be seen there, working with untiring vigour, not to say relish, day after day.

Not a little instruction was given to students outside class-hours. On many occasions it was given while he walked arm in arm with one of his students about the grounds, or it might be at meals, or in conversation late at night in the kitchen of Machen Hall, where he enjoyed weak tea or just simply hot water and milk before bed. Brief 'table talk' from John Murray could make a lasting impression. At dinner one night, a student who was himself to be a professor of Old Testament, once asked him why he had not written more, earlier in his career. For several minutes Murray continued with his meal and then said quite abruptly, 'Because I did not want to have to withdraw what I wrote.' Allan Harman, who gives the anecdote, writes: 'For many of his students the times spent with him in personal conversation were perhaps the times they cherished most. He was ever ready to discuss theological questions and a good deal of Reformed theology was imparted in this way.'

Those who benefited most from Murray are also agreed that they learned as much from his very presence and example as from his actual words. Living as he did among the students, his way of life was constantly open to their observation and they had abundant opportunities to see that his faith and his daily routine formed a harmonious whole. In the words of Calvin Freeman, 'Mr Murray really believed that the Bible was the Word of God—no question about that—and you could sense it in his every breath.' It was as apparent when he was washing his car (a Saturday afternoon practice) as it was in the classroom. Saturday mornings, it should be added, were spent at Faculty meetings where he took an active part.

If there was any particular day which showed the extent to which Murray's pattern of life was not based upon contemporary religious standards it was the Lord's Day. He wholeheartedly believed in the theological principles that lay behind the teaching of the Westminster divines on the holiness of the first day of the week and embraced their high view of the implications of that teaching:

> This sabbath is then kept holy unto the Lord, when men, after a due preparing of their hearts, and ordering of their common affairs beforehand, do not only observe an holy rest all the day from their own works, words, and thoughts about their worldly employments and recreations; but also are taken up the whole time in the public and private exercises of his worship, and in the duties of necessity and mercy (*Westminster Confession of Faith*, XXI:8).

Murray would not enter into general aimless conversation, which had no relevance to spiritual things, on Sundays. If students went with him in his green Plymouth car the fifty minutes' drive to Knox Church on Sunday mornings the conversation would need to be upon Christ and the Bible. Sometimes, if his companion on the journey was of the same spirit, the whole journey might be spent in song, for there were large sections of the Psalter which he could sing by heart to the appropriate tunes. When a student took an opportunity on Sundays to ask such a question as, 'Marked our papers yet, Mr Murray?', he would receive no answer, but, lest there be any misunderstanding, the next day Murray might well take special care to seek out the questioner and walk with him, arm in arm, across the campus. On Sunday evenings he did not return to Knox, but went to the nearby Calvary Orthodox Presbyterian Church; after which he would return alone to his room or eat dinner with one or two like-minded friends. Those who did not share his convictions on the Fourth Commandment were likely to see little of him on the Lord's Day.

Murray's rigorous adherence to what he saw as scriptural principles, it must be said, did not lead him to follow a mere external routine of conscientious duties. Love was the mainspring and, while he would never deviate from principles, his spirituality might lead him to react to situations in a manner that initially took his keen-eyed students by surprise.

Norman Shepherd records the following example:

On one occasion several of us were standing with Professor Murray by the bulletin board in Machen Hall, in which, at that time virtually the whole seminary, exclusive of the library, was housed. As we talked informally, a mother and her four- or five-year-old son came up to us. It was the spring of the year, and the boy had carefully decorated an Easter egg for Professor Murray and now wanted to make the presentation. We watched as the good man accepted the gift with hearty thanks, reinforced with a hug for the child. Pharisees that we were, as soon as mother and child were out of ear-shot, we pounced on the teacher (in a nice way, of course). How could one who was opposed to the observance of religious holiday accept the gift of an Easter egg? Was this not compromise with principle? His answer: 'Receive all things with thanksgiving, asking no questions for conscience sake.' He walked away with the egg, leaving us devastated and properly rebuked.

There is another important lesson which Murray's students observed in him. His life was a witness against any idea that exalted piety means a diminishment of what is truly human. A God-centred life does not mean asceticism or a rejection of those aspects of personality which enrich living with warmth and colour. True Christianity can enter fully into the normal routine things of life. Murray did not want students to talk to him only about theological matters. Morton Smith noticed how he enjoyed and appreciated being included in the ordinary conversation of his students. It was not uncommon for those who shared his table in the Student Dining Club to be 'exhausted from laughter'. The students enjoyed his humour all the more because the things that amused him most were sometimes an indication of his different nationality. Morton Smith recalls how, when one of the students (the Rev. Kennedy Smartt) was serving as a student waiter, he would come to Professor Murray's table each evening with a new joke 'to see how Mr Murray would react'. As Kennedy put it, 'He was trying to find out the difference between the American and British sense of humour.' The kind of joke that John Murray generally enjoyed was one that proceeded dryly until a final, unanticipated 'punch-line' was reached. When, after dinner, someone, speaking for the whole Dining Club, asked, 'Do you have a story for us tonight, Mr Murray?' it would often be a tale of this kind which he would produce. Geoffrey Thomas gives this instance:

I recall the tale of a man who suffered from bells in his ears and lights before his eyes and went for treatment to all the leading medical specialists, but without success. They were all baffled. One day, while nursing his despair, he went out to buy a new shirt and ordered a 14-inch neck. 'Oh sir', said the assistant, 'you need a size 15. If you wear a 14-inch you'll get bells in your ears and lights before your eyes.'

In the opinion of William White, Jr, 'Murray and Van Til, with their strong personalities, really formed the poles around which the world of Westminster was to turn for over forty years.'[1] The statement needs some qualification. Judged in terms of his classroom work, Murray was never a popular communicator. Unlike Van Til, he would no more spend an hour repeating one idea than he would throw a piece of chalk at a sleepy student. To those who had sufficient sympathy with his teaching, and who meant to keep up with him, he was 'an inspiring teacher', but it is probably true that others 'were not up to understanding his lectures'.

By no means were all who passed through Murray's classes moulded to his view of the work of the ministry. Nor is that to be explained exclusively by the demanding nature of his lecturing. It may be said that, to some degree, Murray's spiritual standpoint was not homogeneous with that of the Seminary as a whole, and that this factor must also enter into any evaluation of the limitations of his influence. In Westminster's strong emphasis on the intellectual defence of the Faith, in the many public controversies in which she engaged (with Van Til the principal spokesman), in her stand on 'Christian liberty', and in her opposition to the legalistic 'pietism' of fundamentalism, she needed a strong counter-balance of true piety and spiritual devotion. In so far as the counter-balance was weak, there would be the danger of producing men whose competence for the ministry was largely in the realm of the intellectual and the theoretical, apologists instead of preachers. This danger always exists in theological seminaries, and it increases when the

[1] *Van Til, Defender of the Faith*, p. 102.

courses are offered as an academic discipline to those not motivated by serious commitment to the work of the gospel at home or abroad.[1] At Princeton Seminary, in its best days, the spiritual ethos of the classrooms was constantly strengthened by the total life of the Seminary. As late as 1904, B. B. Warfield could write of Princeton, 'Public means of grace abound in the Seminary.'[2] There were not only daily acts of worship, but a Sabbath morning service in the chapel, a Sabbath afternoon conference on experimental religion, a 'monthly concert for prayer', and similar endeavours 'to preserve a devout spirit and a reverent heart'. The students regularly saw their professors as preachers as well as classroom instructors.

Provision of this kind was much more slender at Westminster and it was a serious loss to the students that they did not hear Murray regularly as a preacher and a leader of public worship. The powerful revivals which had marked Princeton's development at certain points in her history, and raised the student body to new levels of godliness and evangelistic zeal, were not known at Westminster. Instead of the Seminary providing constant *examples* of the truth that preaching is 'theology coming through men who are on fire', there was a degree of disjunction between classroom and pulpit, and this did not have Murray's approval. By word and example he insisted that the first need in those called to preach is that they should be *religious* men: 'Piety must first burn in the individuality of our own hearts and lives. If there is no cultivation of personal piety, the fervour and effectiveness of our ministry will be stultified.'

---

[1] By 1961 the intake at Westminster had risen to 120, and thereafter, as courses were increasingly taken by men and women not entering the ministry, the numbers rose steeply, a development which did not have the support of all the professors.

[2] *Selected Shorter Writings*, vol. 2, p. 476 (a fine article on 'Spiritual Culture in the Seminary').

In this emphasis Murray was certainly admired, and indeed supported by others at Westminster, but if the religious life in the Seminary fell too far short of the standard which he inculcated, at least a part of the explanation may be found in the lack of homogeneity previously mentioned. Few of the institutions mentioned above by Warfield at Princeton survived at Westminster. Too many tended to look upon Murray's piety as something uniquely his own, whereas, in truth, it was the genuine fruit of that type of Calvinistic faith which in other times had pervaded whole seminaries and considerable areas of the church. Indeed there is perhaps no better description of the religion that Murray adorned than words written by another Princeton man, James W. Alexander, on a visit to Scotland in 1851. There, James Alexander says, he found just that type of Christianity in which his own father, Archibald Alexander, first Professor of Theology at Princeton, had delighted:

> The preciousness of it is, that religion is founded on chapter and verse; free from outcry and sanctimony, and even talk about personal feelings, but is so courageous, active and tender, that I am as certain as that I am writing these lines, that I am among the best people on earth. A thousand times have I said to myself, 'O if my father could just for one hour hear these prayers, and observe these fruits of unadulterated Calvinistic seed!'[1]

Such was the Christianity with which John Murray was eminently at home.

Among the several characteristics of Murray's which stand out in his dealings with his students, two in particular must be mentioned.

---

[1] *Forty Years' Familiar Letters of J. W. Alexander,* edited by J. Hall, vol. 2, 1860, p. 157.

The first was *generosity*. Not infrequently this took a financial form. One former student and his wife, who had welcomed Professor Murray to their partially bare manse, were to receive a personal gift from him not long afterwards. 'It came just at about New Year's time. He didn't believe in the observance of Christmas, but that didn't make him less generous at such times of the year. He purchased curtains and a bedspread for our guest room, and we called it the Murray bedroom, though we never informed him of the fact.'

Another student who had just completed his training at Westminster was invited, as a result of John Murray's introduction, to supply the pulpit of Bloor Street Independent Presbyterian Church, Toronto. Visiting Toronto, and noticing that the would-be preacher was still accustomed to the wearing of a flashy suit, scarcely appropriate for the minister of a conservative psalm-singing church, he took him on a visit to a downtown department store. There the young man was made to try on a dark suit of good quality, with which he was, in due course, presented. A protestation of gratitude elicited the reply, 'Freely ye have received, freely give.'

The spirit of generosity was equally evident in Murray's judgment of others. Different generations of students could remember him 'storming down' from 'Murray Heights', with stern countenance, to interrupt a water-fight, or some other form of nonsense going on below, but the offenders never came under his permanent displeasure. He did not expect maturity, and if such conduct was subsequently condemned by others, he could readily find excuses. His kindness in this context was proverbial. Part of the humour of the conversation once alleged to have taken place between two students — 'Which is his glass eye?' 'The kind one!' — was that everyone knew that it was not true. Intolerant of error he certainly was, but in his attitudes towards others he showed a vast amount of sympathy and consideration. No one shunned criticism of fellow

Christians more strongly than he did. In this aspect, as in others, the words of Christ had a governing influence upon his daily walk.

John Murray's second characteristic was *his capacity to inspire affection*. By temperament reserved and shy, it was the degree to which grace possessed him which made his speech and company so attractive to fellow Christians. One of his early students, Lawrence E. Eyres, states it perfectly: 'I can say that he, along with Dr J. Gresham Machen, and very few others of my acquaintance, was a man who, when you knew him, you could not stop just by respecting him for his greatness, but you had to go on to love him. And I did love him, and I love his memory still.'

8

Glimpses of Personal Life

WHEN JOHN MURRAY faced his new class for the first occasion in the fall term of 1954, he was commencing his twenty-fifth teaching year at Westminster. On the day there appeared to be nothing remarkable to mark the occasion; only time was to show that a member of that class was to bring a far-reaching change into his life. The lady was Miss Valerie Y. Knowlton of Augusta, Maine, a graduate of Smith College, who was intent on taking a course in theology before pursuing a career in biology. Almost at once a friendship commenced, which led to a correspondence between them whenever Miss Knowlton was absent from Philadelphia. In the thirteen years which were to pass before their marriage there ensued a long series of letters which, it is clear, became a regular and necessary part of their lives well before his 'Cordially yours' became 'With warmest love'.

The first of these letters, dated 20 June 1955, at once gives a view of the writer scarcely to be imagined by those who only knew the invariable seriousness of his presence in public meetings. The students' summer vacation had begun and we may well imagine with what a wry smile he wrote from his room at the Seminary:

> Few boys remain in Machen Hall; about two, sometimes there are three. May there not be more! I am like the owl: I don't want any one wandering near my secret bower to molest my ancient solitary reign.

Certainly the season of summer at Chestnut Hill, when quietness came to the Seminary and the campus grounds were in their full beauty, was his favourite time of year, and he capitalized on the long days, free from interruption, which he had for writing. Reporting to Valerie that he had been in Grand Rapids, where he had given five lectures and preached twice, he describes his activities as follows:

> I am busy writing and studying and I enjoy the relief from other responsibilities. Last week I wrote one chapter and I am hoping to get another finished this week. I mean, of course, a chapter in a book.[1] If I manage to do approximately that for the remainder of June and July, I will have progressed well as far as quantity is concerned. But oh how the wheels drag sometimes! You know that experience well, don't you?

Yet the writer was, in fact, far from being a recluse and in the same letter he speaks of his reluctant farewell to W. B. Nicholson (a Scottish minister) and his family who had just concluded a period at Westminster. His practical helpfulness at their departure was typical:

> I got the Nicholsons on the train at North Philadelphia on May 25th. I think there were over twenty different pieces of baggage which I had to get packed in my car and then it was a scramble to get them all into the train during the very short time the train was stopped at the station. We got the last in and then immediately the train pulled off. What a relief it was to see that operation completed! *You* would have laughed your lungs out to see it all happen. But oh, they were lovely people. I loved all of them.

[1] Probably his *Principles of Conduct: Aspects of Biblical Ethics*. He had given five lectures on this subject at Fuller Theological Seminary, California, in March 1955, and, as he says in his preface to the published volume, these were 'considerably expanded'.

His next letter was on 1 September 1955:

Dear Valerie,

Thank you for your letter received over a month ago. I was deeply interested in your experiences with two young and charming nephews. You can wax eloquent when you describe the antics of children and your own reactions. I thought you were to have them for a month, but your letter speaks only of a week. I have so many nephews, nieces, grand-nephews and grand-nieces, great grand-nephews and great grand-nieces that, putting them all together, I am not able to keep count . . . I am very well. I had a splendid summer, notwithstanding the heat. I have pretty well completed my first project. The footnotes give me some trouble, for they are books I wish to cite that are not easily found. Gradually I locate some of them in libraries in this area. But how exasperating it is to know of books which provide the information you need for reference and yet not be able to lay hands on them readily. Sometimes you only need them for an hour or a few minutes but you have to go long distances for such books.

I suppose you will be preparing to return to Philadelphia in three weeks. It will be fine to see you again. I hope you got along well with your thesis and got it completed.

Now with best wishes and thanks for your long letter, etc.

The following academic year (1955–56) he was to spend on 'Sabbatical leave' and his main work was to be on his *magnum opus,* the *Commentary on Romans*. With Valerie back in Philadelphia there was no further correspondence until his departure for Scotland at the beginning of November 1955. A letter from the *Empress of Scotland* in the Atlantic reported that there was more than one aspect of the voyage which he was enjoying: 'One day last week we had the most magnificent storm I remember witnessing on the Atlantic.' But what he particularly prized was the presence of his nephew and niece, with 'their lovely baby of 11 months', who were also making the voyage home. Once home at Badbea, a letter of 21 November conveyed fuller news:

Dear Valerie

I got home a week last Friday. Today I had planned to settle down to take care of a pile of correspondence. Your letter came in this morning's mail. Thank you so much for all the news. I had never received such a letter in my life before, I do not believe. It is a diary. You have been living a hectic life, and if this continues you will be a wreck in a few months. So take orders: do not undertake as much ... I cannot vie with you in letter writing. For one thing I do not type and in the coolness and dampness of this climate my hands get cold and I find it so difficult to write when my fingers are some-what 'numb' with cold. But in addition I do not have the capacity for such embryological and psychological disquisitions. But here are some items of news.

The passage over the Ocean was uneventful except for the 'best' storm I had witnessed on the Atlantic. This was my 22nd crossing. My nephew and niece stood it well for neophytes at sea-faring. And the little girl of 11 months was magnificent. I could hardly believe that an infant could so sweetly adjust herself to changing conditions of an entirely new sort. But she did.

We were delayed for about 12 hours by the storm and so we did not call at Greenock, Scotland. We went straight to Liverpool. But it turned out to be an advantage for all of us, I mean our family party.

I stayed for two days in Edinburgh and visited nieces and friends, hunted for books, and bought an umbrella, the first I ever owned. On my way home I left the umbrella in the train. I thought it would be irretrievably lost, but I reported the loss at my destination and lo! the umbrella turned up two or three days later with the postman.

I found all my people marvellously well. My sisters look younger than two years ago; one is 74 and the other 70. Willie my brother looks a bit older, he is 61. My other brother, away from home, looks splendid also; he is 72.

Since coming home I have been doing some manual labour, getting my muscles in shape. You would be surprised at the sort of work I do. Today I was repairing the side-drains on the road leading to the house, so that when floods come they do not take away the gravel on the road. It is grand work to warm one up.

Speaking appointments are now appearing on my horizon. I have to give an address in connection with the Lord's Day Observance Society next Thursday, eleven miles from here. This will be my first appearance in public since coming to this side.

We have had marvellous weather for November, a little frost but no snow, and the last few days have been like April. Yet there is a dampness here which, without central heating, leaves the houses cold. If you know what I mean, it is a raw cold.

I must draw this letter to a close. It is near your dinner time, our supper time, and my brother has come in and looks for his evening meal. I am using the dining room table; it is really our sitting room.

The poor little skunk! I wish I had been there to tend him in his last moments! Perhaps I could have saved him. We have two lovely cats here and a nice sheep and cattle dog. But enough of this tittle-tattle.

Do look after yourself and have plenty of rest at the proper hours. Now with my warmest regards and thanks for your letter, etc.

As the above letter more than hints, conversational letter writing and the communication of 'tittle-tattle' was a new experience for him. To economize in the use of words had long been his habit. He normally undertook correspondence only to answer questions or to supply some basic facts about health, weather and engagements to his friends and family circle. Unable to type, and un-accustomed to use a secretary, he found letter writing a duty rather than a form of relaxation. Valerie's letters were indeed a new experience and he was at least partially successful in breaking away from the more terse letters which hitherto even his best friends might expect to receive. His next two-paged letter of 8 December 1955, contained the following:

> I have had a few preaching engagements in the last two weeks and more are on the way. I was away from home for about three days over what we call the weekend and I shall have the same kind of absence this coming weekend, preaching and visiting. I went away without my spectacles and so I could read little and write practically nothing for these days.[1]
>
> The weather has turned colder in the last few days. I think I am somewhat more adjusted to the damp cold. I still insist on wearing the garb I use in the U.S.A. My sister thinks I should wear long woollen underwear but I am trying to endure with the cotton underwear. Perhaps I shall have to succumb to woollens in this climate as I was wont when young. I always maintain that we men wear too much heavy clothing. Perhaps I am wrong and will smart for it.
>
> I had a letter from Mrs Freeman and have written to her. I do hope she is better.
>
> I have really too much correspondence. My sister was saying last night I would need a postman for myself. A postman is what you call the mailman. In New England you may use the designation 'postman'. Well I must 'post' this letter today so that you get it

---

[56] The lack of spectacles was probably no hindrance to him in conducting services as he could and often did 'read' the Scripture from memory. Congregations never suspected this, although a few observant persons had unnecessary anxious moments.

before you leave for Augusta. Excuse its brevity. I have to go two miles when I wish to 'post' my own letters at the post-office and I either walk or cycle.

Now best wishes, best thanks, and warm regards, etc.

A brief letter of 21 December gave news of frozen water-pipes at Badbea and of his plans to go south shortly for study in libraries. But he could not leave before the major event in the Scottish calendar, as he reports from Edinburgh on 16 January 1956:

At my home we had a fine gathering on New Year's Day, the one day in the year on which we, by a long tradition, have celebrations. There were 21 of us in all, most of us related in one way or another, though a few friends were outside our family circle. But we should have had the family reunion more complete. Several were not there who wanted to be there.

I hope you have had a successful mid-year examination period. I have had letters from three of my colleagues recently and they seem to be encouraged and happy. I have had no news from the Freemans for a while. I do hope they are well.

I have no permanent address at present except my home address, from which my mail is regularly forwarded. I scarcely know where I may be from one day to another, though at present I am most hospitably and comfortably entertained by friends here in Edinburgh. Only, I feel like a mean 'tramp' imposing on them. I am such an independent old fox that I hate to be a burden on any. I would, of course, be willing to pay high-class lodging rates. But I dread to mention this lest they might be offended. So there it goes.

As far as his studies for *Romans* were concerned he was only partially successful in finding books that he needed, and he therefore extended his search to the libraries in his old University of Glasgow, from where he wrote on 7 February 1956:

Dear Valerie

I received your letter in a batch of mail that was forwarded to my address in the West of Scotland, near Glasgow. I came to Glasgow about ten days ago and I did find some things I had been looking for, much to my satisfaction. But I have not found Glasgow quite as rewarding as Edinburgh. The reason for that may be that I went to the latter first and I have no need of looking here for the books I found there. I shall probably go home at the end of this week for a week or two and attend to work which I can do there without a great deal of trouble.

I hope you are now back at Seminary and that your mother is really better. You had a long absence from your friends at Westminster.

I have had no correspondence from Philadelphia for some time now, except a note from Brown, telling me about his baby.

I have another grand-niece. My nephew Alexander and his wife have another daughter, born about two weeks ago. This is their second child.

I am really well. I am surprised that I have been able to keep so well under the conditions of confinement in libraries, especially when a great many of the volumes I use give off a good deal of the black dust which, as you know, collects on books that have not been in use. The dust is more like soot. I am of the opinion that some of these books have not been perused for a generation, perhaps more. I found in Glasgow the book I had been particularly anxious to lay my hands on. When I saw it, I could not contain myself. I had to express my jubilation to the library girls at the desk and told them I was afraid, before that moment, that I might have to go to the Continent to find it. This edition was 1585 but there may have been an earlier edition. It isn't the date that interested me so much as the contents.

We had a very cold spell here last week and on Saturday thousands of water-pipes were burst in this city. They were frozen on Friday and the thaw on Saturday caused a lot of inconvenience.

By the end of March 1956 he had largely completed his research and was needing his own books and notes which were still at Westminster. He therefore booked a return passage on the *Queen Elizabeth*, due to sail from Southampton on 12 April. But, as always, it was a wrench to leave Badbea, as he explains to Valerie on 27 March:

> I shall be sad leaving home, especially parting with my two sisters. They are wonderfully well, but one is 74 and the other 70. My brother at home here is 62, at least approaching that. And this is one of the most beautiful spots in the world with the loch in front and the hills surrounding on all sides. Badbea is a small district with only two houses, ours and a neighbour's. There were three houses, but one is now a ruin.
>
> I have had good weeks since I wrote you last, but I do not expect to have much continuous study now until I return to the U.S.A.

Once back at Westminster, and with no teaching schedule until October 1956, he pressed on with the work on Romans. On account of the poor health of her mother in Maine, Valerie was not with the student body when they re-assembled for Commencement in May. He therefore wrote to her on 14 May:

> I suppose that the fine weather that has struck us must be extending some of its warmth to Augusta. It was 91 on the official reading in this area today. I enjoyed it greatly. The library was just the right temperature for me, probably around 75.
>
> Tomorrow and Wednesday are the busy days of the Commencement season here. I plan to isolate myself completely and I shall likely go to Princeton for these two days so that I shall not be

interrupted by endless intrusions. You may wonder, but when I want to study that is the only alternative.

The same letter contains news of his new car, 'a Plymouth with push-button transmission', and concludes with a quip in response to an observation from Valerie that the aroma of a booklet which he had sent her from Badbea suggested that he had blown too much tobacco smoke over it:

> I shall try the stunt of giving you a whiff of tobacco. I am not sure that was what infected the booklet. It might have been peat smell from my home. Peat is what we burn, and it leaves a pleasant and distinctive odour on clothing which hangs around the living room. The booklet may have contracted some of that, but, of course, there is plenty of tobacco around my habitat wherever it happens to be.[1]

The weeks that followed provided few events to report until after his return from the General Assembly of the Orthodox Presbyterian Church, which that year met in Denver in July. It had meant a considerable journey by train. A letter of 11 August 1956 reports:

> I got back from Denver a week last Thursday. My journeys by train to and from Denver were quite restful but the Assembly was fairly strenuous. On the whole it was a good Assembly, not so much for what it did as for the actions it refused to take. The general attitude to the new form of government was gratifying, although the Assembly postponed action for another year, and recommitted the proposed revision to the committee for further study. Of that committee I happen to be a member and I was pleased that the

---

[1] Scottish Presbyterians and many English Nonconformists (e.g. C. H. Spurgeon) never regarded the use of tobacco as contrary to Scripture. Had they possessed the evidence which we now have on the connection between nicotine and lung cancer they might have desisted.

Assembly turned down several proposals which would have meant the rejection in important particulars of the revisions which our committee had proposed.

On Saturday afternoon, which was an afternoon free from Assembly business, several of us drove to the top of Mount Evans (14,260 feet). It was superbly grand. That is the highest altitude I have ever attained on *terra firma*. I felt just fine at that altitude and could climb the few remaining hundred feet from the parking lot without any trouble. Some people feel miserable at that altitude, as you know.

I am now hard at work again and I am not dissatisfied with my progress. I have been working since February on Romans. As you may know, I am supposed to publish a commentary on the same one of these years. This is the first time I have been able to concentrate on this task for any length of time. I hope to continue until it is complete, *the Lord willing*. I have got to enjoy the work but sometimes progress is very slow. One word or clause can hold you up so long. So often the precise force of a conjunction, like γάρ or ὅτι, is difficult to determine.

Now I do hope you are well and that you have had a good rest at your cottage on the lake. Our summer has been comfortably cool, so different from 1955, with abundance of rain. All the way to Denver the crops looked good except in the vicinity of Denver.

By the Fall of 1956 when his old teaching schedule was renewed with 72 students, Valerie was back in Philadelphia and no more letters were necessary until the summer of the following year. As was common in the years when he was not home in Scotland, the summer of 1957 found him visiting and preaching among his friends at Chesley, Ontario. It was the last occasion on which he was to be with William Matheson, the pastor of that congregation, whom John Murray so highly esteemed. On 30 December 1957, again from Chesley (where he often went for a short visit over the New Year period), he wrote:

> I miss my dear friend here. In both services yesterday I made reference to the fidelity of their deceased pastor and tried to press home the necessity of maintaining the witness which he so faithfully bore.

Many were the letters written from Chesley to Valerie at different periods and there is much similarity about the news that they convey. There were a number of reasons why the visits to Chesley meant so much to him. He found among the Christians of that part of Ontario a spirit of piety, a consciousness of the privileges and duties of Sabbath observance, and a high view of the worship of God in psalms, prayer, and sacraments, which was all too rare even among the Presbyterian witness in Philadelphia. Writing after a communion season at Lochalsh on one occasion he says to Valerie: 'I think I feel most at home here and in Chesley of all the places I visit.' These congregations also afforded to him a fuller opportunity to share both in preaching and in pastoral care than was possible in Philadelphia. He ever cherished the conviction that the great object of the work at Westminster was to help prepare men for work at the parish level and he considered it to be an important part of his own personal duty as a minister of the gospel to fulfil his own calling in that respect whenever he was permitted. He therefore prized the providence which gave him these openings among the Ontario congregations, and his care for the services and for the people could scarcely have been greater had he been their settled pastor.

On 26 May 1958, he writes to Valerie from Canada:

> I got to Chesley late on Saturday night after spending some nine hours in Toronto and four and a half on the train from Toronto to Chesley. Yesterday was a pleasant day with two services at 11.00 a.m.

and 7.00 p.m. The attendances were quite good for this small congregation, about 30 in the morning and 40 at night. It is a most pleasant little church in which to preach and there seem to be a goodly number of hungry souls. Being without a minister now for six months they appreciate preaching all the more. I *tried* to preach on *Rom.* 4:9–11 in the morning and on *John* 18:37 at night. I plan to go to Lochalsh on Thursday for services each day until Monday. As you know there are five days of services in connection with communion in these congregations.

The next week a letter contained additional news on these services:

If you have been praying for me on this mission, your prayers have been answered, at least to the extent of my being wonderfully helped in the last five days at the daily services. I scarcely knew how I was going to get through. But hitherto the Lord has helped.

From the same address he writes in July 1959:

Last week I spent four days visiting the people of these congregations, two days in the Lochalsh area and two days further south. I got around practically all the people in these areas. I am visiting the people here now and I plan to go to Newton on Thursday and Toronto on Friday. I have done a great deal of driving. I shall probably have driven well over 2,000 miles before I return to Philadelphia.

Mrs Matheson is awfully good to me: she treats me the way my sisters do.

I saw an old lady last week aged 102. But she is very frail, now bedridden, and wasted to a shadow. When I saw her four years ago, she was quite well and in possession of all her faculties. But she will not live much longer.

In 1961 he again drove to Chesley and planned his route to include calls upon a number of people for whom he had a pastoral concern. They included a mentally-ill man in hospital at Willard, New York, with whom he stayed an hour, although, 'This time I could not understand a word he said.' In another place he stopped to see a mother and little girl who had formerly lived in Chesley and belonged to the congregation. Far from being reticent with children, or awkward with babies, there was no company that John Murray more highly enjoyed. Happily, events did not often occur such as one, which he reports to Valerie, during his 1961 summer visit to Chesley:

> Last night I was preaching here and we had a sharp storm during the service. All lights went out. But there was still enough daylight. There was a baptism after. I never had such an experience. The little boy roared all the time. I think he got a scare of some kind towards the end of the sermon. It was awfully hard on the parents and on me also.
>
> There have been good congregations at the services, that is, good for these churches. Last night there were about 60.
>
> I plan to visit in the southern parts for some days this week and return on Friday.

Many aspects of John Murray's character emerge in the letters which were sent in increasing numbers to Valerie. He was child-like in his unconscious freedom from any sense of self-importance. It never disturbed him, for example, to be asked to undertake a long and difficult journey to speak, perhaps, to a small number of people. The possible size of a meeting would make no difference to his response to such invitations: if it was possible, he would accept. Even when he sometimes met with thoughtless inconsideration it did not ruffle him, as, for instance, when on one occasion he agreed to make the tedious journey from Badbea to speak in

Edinburgh only to be informed on his arrival 'that it must be limited to about 20 minutes'! His only comment to Valerie was: 'A lot can be said in 20 minutes. But that is not my talent.' An awareness of the privilege and responsibility of any service rendered in Christ's name possessed him to a high degree and explains why *his* attitude to his labours was often so different from that of those who richly benefited from them. 'I was thoroughly disgusted with my lecture, though the topic was so important', he writes after an address in the Town Hall, Inverness. Or, again, after taking services in Free St Columba's, Edinburgh: 'I enjoyed the communion but am also filled with self-reproach and can only plead, "God be merciful to me."'

The one thing which was almost sure to provoke his spirit in his dealing with others was when he considered that he was needlessly kept awake at night because of the noise of those whose hours of rest were far less regular than his own. In part, it was in wisdom gained from experience that he made his objections. To close friends he often mentioned with some regret the nights spent in conversation as a young man. Although the conversations had been both profitable and enjoyable from an intellectual standpoint, he was not convinced that such use of time was entirely justified. He never forgot he was a pastor and spared no diligence in caring for the best interests of others. Consequently generations of students in Machen Hall became accustomed to admonitions on this subject, which varied in their severity according to the degree of the offence!

Even fellow ministers at the Leicester Conference in England were once stopped in the midst of a loud midnight discussion by the daunting appearance of the professor in night attire, with pocket watch in hand raised for their inspection and reflection! The bedrooms where the Conference was held had not been arranged to meet the differing needs of sleepers and talkers. On

John Murray's corridor the 'talkers' never attempted to win after that memorable occasion!

Once, after a busy day taken up with church affairs in New England, John Murray booked in at the Statler Hilton in Boston where he wrote to Valerie before retiring for the night. To her surprise, a few days later another letter (3 April 1961) conveyed the news that the Boston hotel had prematurely lost their guest:

> I did not stay in Boston after all. Believe it or not, I settled down in the Statler and went to bed. But it was so noisy, I could not sleep. At midnight I got up, complained to the desk, and said I was going to leave. I cancelled my reservation, dressed again, handed in my key, went across the street to the bus depot and took the bus that left for New York at 1.15 a.m. I got to New York at 6.30, got a bus in a few minutes for Philadelphia, and was in Philadelphia at the depot a few minutes after 9.00 a.m. I got snatches of sleep and did not feel too exhausted. I got to the Seminary about 11.00 a.m., having leisurely breakfasted before taking the subway.

Nothing was more repugnant to John Murray than a parade of 'spirituality' or of religious sentiments. Comment on spiritual subjects was not common in letters and when it occurred it was brief and to the point. Thus, in an early letter (2 July 1956) he writes from a 'very quiet' Westminster to Valerie at her home in Maine:

> I can well sympathise with you in respect to the difficulties of which you told me in conversation once and to which you referred in your letter of over two weeks ago. I am not in a position to assess all the circumstances. But I just wonder how your deference to the prejudices and feelings of others squares with our Lord's word that whosoever loveth father or mother more than me is not worthy of me. I cannot refrain from the question and my respect for you prompts me all the more to it.

In another letter from Badbea on 28 July 1958, he gives news of his recent speaking engagements in London. Commenting on Valerie's vacation activities (reported in her last letter), he adds, 'I don't know how heart or conscience could stand the strain or tolerate the day of Sabbath travel through Ontario.' By 11 August he had a reply from Valerie and it led him to take up his pen at once with the following paragraph:

> Your letter of Tuesday last has just arrived. I have just turned to 2 Corinthians 7:8-11, for it immediately occurred to me that this paralleled your reaction to my remark *re* Sabbath travel. I sin, too, but I wish I could repent, as you apparently do. I can, however, appreciate your chagrin. At our last General Assembly I made a remark, or series of remarks, from the floor that was unfair to a fellow commissioner. I made public apology to the Assembly and private apology to the person injured. He readily forgave me, as a Christian gentleman. But oh! what pain that error gave me; it still makes me smart when I think of it. Well, the fruit of repentance is always after the pattern of verse 11 in the passage cited above.

How typical these words were of their writer's spirit! When he counselled others it was as one who himself pursued holiness of heart and life. It was, perhaps, partly on account of his reserve as a Highland Scot, and partly on account of his view of the Christian life, that he *said* little about feelings in spiritual experience, yet, as his friends well knew, he felt keenly and deeply. When Valerie's grandmother died, whom she had helped her mother to nurse in their home at Augusta, Maine, John wrote at once on 28 December 1959:

> Your letter of Thursday has just been received. But your 'phone call of last evening has informed me of the change that occurred since you wrote. I want to convey to you my deep sympathy and also to

your mother. I wondered all last week how your grandmother was. Now she is no longer with you. Before this letter reaches you the funeral will be over. How real is death, and how dismal except as its darkness is illumined by the hope of resurrection to life! It is as we look death squarely in the face that the grace and power of the Saviour take on new meaning. How tawdry are all human attempts to dress it up! The light and faith of Jesus alone can cast a halo of joy and hope around it. Blessed are the dead who die in the Lord, and only they! There is nothing that any person can place between himself or herself and the damnation that sin demands, but the merit, blood, righteousness, mediatorship, and intercession of the risen and glorified Redeemer. May this experience be for you and all yours, the means of grace to this end of realizing how precious is He who Himself is the resurrection and the life. I know that your own thoughts gravitate irresistibly in this direction. May you know as never before the presence of the Saviour and the comfort of His promises. 'I will never leave thee, nor forsake thee' is His promise.

I may leave for Ontario on Wednesday. I finished the three larger articles. One other I may get finished tomorrow, and then three shorter ones remain. But perhaps I can leave them until January. If I go to Ontario I shall be fully occupied with visiting and speaking and may not get back until January 6.

Do accept my warm regards. I hope you rest now. Your mother will need you in Augusta for two weeks.

I am very well. The building has been delightfully quiet since last Wednesday. The dense fog is still with us.

P.S. I shall have no forwarding address in Ontario. I shall only be a few days in one place. And my itinerary is all so uncertain, besides.

The reason, of course, for the tranquillity at Westminster was the occurrence of the 'festive season' which had, as usual, left the

Seminary deserted at this time. He enjoyed those December days for reasons rather different from the common ones, as he explains to Valerie in a letter written on 'Christmas Eve' the previous year:

> Here I am alone in the library and apparently everyone has gone from Machen Hall until Friday morning. Now it is 9.30 p.m. on Wednesday. You may think this dismal. Well, I love it. It is a delightful change from the usual stir. I have had two good days in the Library. Monday was taken up with committee meetings, forenoon and afternoon. I hope to be here all day tomorrow. I have not even accepted a dinner engagement for what they call 'Christmas'. I hate the whole business.

From all John Murray's letters to Valerie it is clear that there was no activity which he enjoyed so much as his vacations at Badbea. A sense of the sheer splendour of the surroundings never seemed to leave him and allusions to it abound in his correspondence. Writing from the table in the 'parlour' (which he made his den whenever he was home), he says in one letter: 'Since I last wrote we have had some magnificent weather and two days of rain. Yesterday was grand and this morning is a dead calm. The loch is like glass and the shadows from the hills and trees on the opposite side are perfect. The heather is now in bloom and so the hills are clothed in purple. Since beginning this letter I have looked out at the loch and hills beyond, I don't know how many times.' 'Last night', he writes again, 'I went up the hill at 10.30 to view the hills: perfect visibility and the glow was superb. I never saw anything more gorgeous.' Sunset an hour before midnight is not uncommon in the North of Scotland in mid-summer. He found the early morning views from Badbea equally entrancing.

Next to his family and the scenery it was in the manual, farming activity at Badbea that he revelled. Agriculture itself interested him: He believed that there was perhaps nowhere in the world 'where agriculture is more intensively and scientifically carried on than within fifteen miles of my home'. But it was the strenuous activity and the animals which appealed to him chiefly. There was always an abundance of work to be done on their croft, which was run by his brother William. Besides thirty acres of arable land William bred cattle and sheep, for which there was good hill pasture. Those who had only seen John Murray address a public meeting in his dark, well-pressed suit, or lecture students in theology, would have been amazed at his changed role at Badbea! He cut hay, dug ditches, milked cows, and drove sheep with a sheep dog, as though he had never done anything else in his life. His physique was unusually strong and he was never back at Badbea for long before his muscles were hardened and the skin of his hands like leather. The present writer's first sight of him at his own home was when he was some sixty years of age and standing, vigorously swinging a scythe, in the field between Badbea and the loch below!

Sometimes he seems to have felt that he loved Badbea too much. He quotes to Valerie the testimony of a Highlander of an earlier generation who, amid the poverty which prevented him from mending the leaking roof of his earthly dwelling, saw it as an act of God's providence which enabled him to say, 'It will not be so hard to leave it.' In contrast, Badbea had almost no imperfections. On occasions the dilapidated 'byre', which somewhat 'marred' the view toward the east, bothered him, and there were times when the sheep, tormented with 'midges' (small flies), broke his sleep with their bleating ('I went out after them at 2.30 a.m. to try to get them away from the proximity of the house'!) but these things hardly fulfilled his thought that 'there has to be something to spoil the pleasure of the spot'! After reflections on this attachment to Badbea, he concludes: 'Some people, who are not prejudiced as I am, think this spot to be the most beautiful they have ever seen.' He knew they were right!

9

The Wider Influence

PERSONAL FACTORS and spiritual convictions alike prevented John Murray from restricting his interests to the work within Westminster Seminary. Unlike Warfield at Princeton, whose activity beyond the Seminary was very much restricted by the infirmity of his wife, he had no home responsibilities in the United States, and his temperament was such that he enjoyed travelling and meeting people further afield. In addition, the closeness of his ties with his family meant that he was usually found in Scotland every other summer after the close of the Second World War.

Certain spiritual convictions also led him to place much importance upon work outside the Seminary. He took a high view of a Christian's duty to be a member of the most faithful church that is to be found and to support that church with sacrificial vigour. In his own case that duty led him to give a great deal of time and energy to the witness of the Orthodox Presbyterian Church. Whenever possible he was present in the meetings of the Presbytery of New York and New England, and he frequently served in the General Assembly of the Church.

Cornelius Van Til recalls how when Murray was Moderator of the General Assembly he once strikingly manifested a trait which was so characteristic of him, displaying no respect of persons in dealing with men of social distinction or of academic rank but treating all with the same fairness and impartiality:

He allowed no one, old or young, however eloquent, to exceed the time allotted him by the Robert's *Rules of Order*. His facial expression revealed his determination that, in the Church of Christ above all, no one must be given prior recognition because he had come early and usurped a front seat and spoke with a loud voice, and that no one should be ignored because he sat in the back row and spoke with a soft voice.

In particular John was out to do justice to the non-teaching elder, the man with little or no formal education, the man whose manner was plebeian and whose diction was that of the unlearned. This man might very well have a point to make. Sanctified common sense was not to be despised. At any rate, the 'common man' had his rights, and if the audience snickered or even laughed when he 'murdered' the King's English, the moderator's gavel came down with vigour.

Murray also played a leading part in many church committees, as, for example, the important Committee on Foreign Missions to which he belonged for a quarter of a century. Occasionally committees of short duration were set up to elucidate and report upon particular problems. His work as secretary of the Committee on Local Evangelism has already been mentioned. As Chairman of the Committee on Texts and Proof Texts (in respect of various editions of the *Westminster Confession*), he submitted to the General Assembly a text derived from the original manuscript written by Cornelius Burgess in 1646 with the proof-texts revised. The purity of the text of the *Westminster Confession* had long been a matter of great interest to him; he gave much time to the subject and it was the theme of the first book review he contributed to the *Westminster Theological Journal* in 1939.[1]

---

[1] See *Collected Writings*, vol. 3, p. 291.

A special committee of far-reaching importance was elected by the General Assembly to revise the denomination's Form of Government and Book of Discipline. As Chairman of this Committee, which continued its work for more than ten years, John Murray exercised a major influence in formulating the revisions that were recommended to the Assembly. In an article in *The Presbyterian Guardian* (15 September 1954) he shows why some of the recommended changes were needed and emphasizes the necessity for church government to be grounded upon the warrant of the New Testament, that is to say, upon the authority of Christ. Popular thought which influences church practice, as for example, the idea that 'the minister' stands apart from elders, is therefore not to be countenanced:

> The committee has endeavoured to carry out the presbyterian principle consistently. If the presbyterian form of government is government by presbyters, then all who are presbyters in the New Testament sense exercise this function of government on a parity with one another. The teaching elder, often called the minister, does not have any priority or superiority in respect of ruling in the church of God. Ruling elders and teaching elders have equal authority in this matter of rule. This is exemplified in the committee's version by the provision stated expressly in Chapter IX, Section 3: 'It is not requisite that the pastor should be moderator of the session'. The committee seeks to guard against an unwholesome clericalism which has frequently crept in and which has tended to rehabilitate practical hierarchicalism even in the presbyterian tradition. This emphasis upon the parity of presbyters in the rule of the church should minister to the correction of a widespread evil, the failure of ruling elders to appreciate and perform the responsibilities that are theirs in the government of the church. This applies with the session oftentimes, but it is particularly apparent in the higher judicatories.

The work of the Orthodox Presbyterian Church in revising its Form of Government and Book of Discipline, ought to be far better known than it is. As the above quotation shows, it touches upon issues of general importance in all the Reformed churches today.

Occasionally John Murray's views were not those of the majority of a committee upon which he was serving. This occurred, notably, when the Committee on Song in Public Worship presented its report to the General Assembly in 1947, and John Murray, together with William Young, submitted an eight-page Minority Report, detailing reasons why the Book of Psalms should be held to be *the* divinely appointed hymn book for the Christian church. The minority view was not accepted by the Assembly.

For a number of years the Orthodox Presbyterian Church was engaged in a controversy about the incomprehensibility of God, the place of the created intellect, and the free offer of the gospel. Of the complexities of these debates, which culminated in the years 1946–8, it is not now practicable to undertake an analysis. Suffice it to say that John Murray's theological contributions were outstanding. In the report submitted to the Fifteenth General Assembly in 1948, it was he who supplied the formulation of the doctrine of God's incomprehensibility, the statements from the classic Reformed theologians, and much of the exegesis on which the conclusions were based. It was he also who was the author of the important section on 'The Free Offer of the Gospel', later reprinted in a pamphlet which had a wide distribution.[1] The pamphlet says, 'The study was prepared by the Rev. Professors John Murray and Ned B. Stonehouse.' Dr Stonehouse's name was added because he, as a member of the Committee on Doctrine, did offer editorial suggestions. But the author was John Murray.

---

[1] See *Collected Writings*, vol. 4, pp. 113–32, and, in booklet form, *The Free Offer of the Gospel,* Edinburgh, Banner of Truth, 2001 (32 pp.) .

Even when Murray did not belong to a committee, his judgment was not infrequently sought on vexed issues. In 1956, when two sub-committees of the Committee on Christian Education, struggling to prepare a report for the General Assembly on the question of pictorial representations of Christ, had come to different conclusions, the matter was referred to John Murray. With his customary clarity of thought and language, his reply in three pages demonstrated why such representations ought not to be employed. The crux of his argument was that every thought and impression of Christ ought to be accompanied with the reverence that belongs to worship. All truth concerning Christ presented in Scripture is in order to worship. 'A picture of Christ, if it serves any useful purpose, must evoke some thought or feeling respecting him and, in view of what he is, this thought or feeling will be worshipful.' Yet such worship would not be based upon the revelatory data of Scripture (containing as it does no descriptions of Christ's physical features) but upon a human figment. It was his judgment that the presence of pictures of Christ in places of worship 'only demonstrates how insensitive we readily become to the commandments of God and to the inroads of idolatry. May the Churches of Christ be awake to the deceptive expedients by which the arch-enemy ever seeks to corrupt the worship of the Saviour.'

John Murray's influence went, moreover, far beyond the borders of his own denomination. He could not view with equanimity the division of the church into denominations, and he repudiated the argument that, because the unity of the invisible church is spiritual and has at its centre the unity of believers with Christ, therefore the unity of the visible church is of comparative insignificance. His understanding of the New Testament allowed him to accept no distinction of this kind between the church invisible and the church visible: he considered that the spiritual unity of believers with Christ heightens the imperative need for unity of confession and testimony in the world. His convictions on this theme are set down in various articles, of which one of the most interesting, 'The Biblical Basis for Ecclesiastical Union', appears to have been written in connection with the uniting of the Bloor Street East Church in Toronto with the Free Presbyterian Church of Ontario. Though it was but a small achievement in unity, judged merely by the sizes of the churches involved, it meant much to John Murray. Ever since 1926 he had continued to visit with unfailing regularity the Ontario congregations, served by his friend William Matheson of Chesley; in the 1940s for a time, when the Bloor Street congregation was pastorless, he had served as Moderator, and in 1952 he received a call to the pastorate at Bloor Street, a call which he could not have found it easy to decline.

In the article referred to above he writes:

1. The fragmentation and consequent lack of fellowship, harmony, and co-operation which appear on the ecclesiastical scene are a patent contradiction of the unity exemplified in that to which Jesus referred when he said, 'as thou, Father, art in me and I in thee'.

2. The purpose stated in Jesus' prayer, 'that the world may believe that thou hast sent me', implies a manifestation observable by the world. Jesus prays for a visible unity that will bear witness to the world. The mysterious unity of believers with one another must come to visible expression so as to be instrumental in bringing conviction to the world.

This same concern came to expression in his relationships with other churches in the United States.

When, in 1956, the Synod of the Christian Reformed Church took the initiative in seeking to establish closer relations with the Orthodox Presbyterian Church, John Murray was active in urging an appropriate response from his own denomination. He had many personal friendships with ministers and students of the

Christian Reformed Church and was no stranger to their College and Seminary in Grand Rapids. In an article on the need for closer relationships with the Christian Reformed Church in *The Presbyterian Guardian* (25 April 1959) he wrote:

> It would be unrealistic, of course, to fail to take account of the differences that exist between the two denominations . . . The differences must be frankly faced and ways and means explored of solving them . . . But the ultimate objective and the obligation arising from it should not be obscured or overlooked. There is the necessity which cannot be suppressed that the unity which belongs to the church as the body of Christ should be brought to expression in every phase of the church's function and, therefore, in government and discipline . . . The church is not ours; it is the church of Christ. And nothing underlies the sanctity of the cause to which we are committed and the obligations inherent in this commitment more than the fact that the church is the body of Christ, the fulness of him that filleth all in all.[1]

In this same concern for wider Christian unity, Murray also gave himself to the strengthening of the witness of the Reformed Ecumenical Synod. He was present at the Synod's meeting in Edinburgh in 1953, and thereafter served on a committee appointed to report on the inspiration of the Scriptures; the forty-page report which this committee presented to the Synod which met in South Africa in 1958, with its insistence upon the doctrine of inerrancy, is a fine statement of the belief which Murray was so jealously concerned to guard. But the fact that the same doctrine

---

[1] For a fuller treatment of this subject see 'The Nature and Unity of the Church' in *Collected Writings*, vol. 2, pp. 321-35. As his trenchant article, 'Co-operation in Evangelism' (*Collected Writings*, vol. 1, pp. 152-62) shows, it was never, of course, his view that the interests of unity, even for the purpose of evangelism, have priority over the interests of truth.

of Scripture was not so unequivocally upheld by the Synod, while causing him regret, did not prevent him from contributing further to its work. A committee on Eschatology had been appointed in 1949, but ten years passed without any report being produced. Finally the committee was reconstituted under the chairmanship of Jim Grier, and he and John Murray together brought out the excellent thirty-one page report which was presented to the Fifth Reformed Ecumenical Synod, meeting at Grand Rapids in 1963. This Synod, at which he was elected 'First Assessor', was the last at which John Murray was present, but his written work for Synod committees continued, and as late as the summer of 1970, with the compression of which he was a master, he wrote sixteen pages for the consideration of committee colleagues on the subject of 'Office in the Church'.[1]

* * * * *

As noted earlier, John Murray thought of himself all his life as a Britisher, and we turn now to make brief comment on his influence here in his native island. During his visits home in the 1930s his opportunities for usefulness were limited; the pulpits of the Free Presbyterian Church were not open to him and his associations with the Free Church of Scotland were comparatively undeveloped. These were the only two denominations committed to the Reformed Faith in the Scottish Highlands. When on occasions, he undertook to speak in public halls, under no denominational auspices, it is still remembered that the meetings were crowded. After the Second World War his contacts in the Free Church of Scotland quickly multiplied and his services were eagerly sought at the communion seasons in many Highland congregations, including the church at Creich. It was a testimony both

[1] *See Collected Writings*, vol. 2, pp. 357–65.

of personal affection, and of regard for the work in which John Murray was engaged at Westminster, when Dr John MacLeod of Edinburgh invited him in 1946 to take some of the cream of his library back to the library at Westminster Seminary. Two years later John Murray shared in the simple family service that took place at the burial of this Free Church leader.

On occasions when he was home from America such evangelical organizations as the Inter-Varsity Fellowship (now UCCF), The Lord's Day Observance Society, and, in later years, the Reformation Translation Fellowship, were all eager to employ his services in Scotland.

If the impression of the present writer is correct, John Murray's first speaking engagement in England did not come until as late as 1953. At that date his name was little known in the south of the United Kingdom, even among evangelical Christians.[1] The explanation is that Presbyterianism, as a vital force, was dead in England by that date and in the capital city, where the *Westminster Confession* was drawn up, there was only one figure who was commonly recognized as believing and preaching the doctrines which it contained. The prevailing ethos of English Evangelicalism (a modified form of the Fundamentalist ethos of America) and that of John Murray were alien to each other. In 1953, however, Dr Martyn Lloyd-Jones (the London preacher to whom we have just referred), as President of the Evangelical Library, invited John Murray to give the Annual Library lecture on 'Reformation Principles'. The same year, Murray also gave at Cambridge the Tyndale Lecture under the auspices of the Theological Students' Fellowship (a branch of the Inter-Varsity Fellowship) on 'The Covenant

---

[1] When a lecture by him on 'The Presbyterian Form of Church Government' was published by a recently formed Evangelical Presbyterian Fellowship in London in 1958 it was considered necessary to explain that 'although Prof Murray has spent many years in the U.S.A., he actually hails from Scotland'.

of Grace'. A Summer School for theological students was meeting at Tyndale House, Cambridge, at the same time as this lecture was delivered and Murray's contributions to that School were memorable. Edwin King recalls how he and others 'found the lecture on "the Covenant" heavy going, but', he continues,

> his paper on 'Limited Atonement' was a classic, and a child could have followed it. He was obviously in his element, and in my opinion I have never heard anyone who could better him on the theme. Of course, as soon as he had finished, the sniping commenced. Apart from the chairman (Dr Lloyd-Jones) there were few there who were not concerned to defend a universal atonement. Not without considerable excitement it was urged that Murray's belief would inhibit evangelism; that it would kill enthusiasm for witness and concern for the lost! After listening quietly to such objections, John Murray rose to his feet, moved in front of the table, and began to pace up and down the centre aisle between the chairs on which we were sitting. His eyes gleamed, and I could tell he had been stirred by the carnality of it all. In his dark sombre clothes and sallow appearance he was, to me, a most moving sight. Then, very deliberately and slowly, he began: 'I can honestly say I have never heard the gospel preached more sweetly and savingly to sinners, nor with more saving power, than it was when I heard it as a boy up in . . .' I could not catch the name of the place, but I knew he was referring to the Highlands of Scotland. The meeting was at once sobered down, and he then began to reminisce about the old preachers, how passionately they held to each of the 'five points' and how God had owned their ministries to the quickening and awakening of sinners.

Murray was next in London, again at the invitation of Dr Lloyd-Jones, to give the Campbell Morgan Bible Lecture at Westminster Chapel in June 1958. By this date a remarkable resurgence of interest in the Reformed Faith was occurring in England and, notably, through influences stemming from Westminster Chapel where Dr Lloyd-Jones, who belonged to the Welsh Calvinistic Methodist tradition, had ministered since 1938. Partly as a result of these influences, a specifically Reformed publishing house, the Banner of Truth Trust, had been founded by D. J. W. Cullum and the present writer in 1957 and, in the first announcement of the works which it planned to print, the new publishers expressed their indebtedness to the counsel of three men, Dr Lloyd-Jones, Jim Grier, and John Murray. Professor Murray wrote commendations for two of the first titles to appear (Charles Hodge's *Princeton Sermons* and *Jonathan Edwards' Select Works*, volume 1). Through the work of the Banner of Truth Trust, in which he thus shared from the outset, John Murray developed a much closer connection with the situation in England, and within a short time, he came to have a strong influence on a number of the younger ministers. These men, who had begun to read deeply in Calvin, Owen, and Edwards, deplored how the older generation, with few exceptions, had treated their writings as non-existent.

The eclipse of Calvinism, which Spurgeon had predicted so forcefully eighty years before, had long become a reality. But in the providence of God, John Murray's coming to England coincided with the re-awakening already mentioned, and it was inevitable that those who had felt the power of the doctrines of grace should gravitate to him.

Their reading and, in many instances, the influence of Dr Lloyd-Jones, had taught them that contemporary Christianity needed to pass through a revolution if it was to be readapted to the Word of God. John Murray, then in his full maturity, brought powerful corroboration and gave further momentum to the thinking that was bringing about a new departure in English evangelicalism.

Very much at the centre of this new thinking was the belief that the lack of conviction of sin, observable in the church, and the absence of an appreciation of the majesty of God, were sure signs of the need for a true revival. But such a revival could not be expected until attention was addressed to certain spiritual realities all-too-commonly neglected in modern preaching, not only in Arminian circles but also in churches of the Reformed tradition. A change was needed in the pulpit. John Murray had spoken on this theme to the alumni of Westminster Seminary in 1952 in an address entitled 'Some Necessary Emphases in Preaching'. The first missing emphasis, he observed, was, 'the ministry of judgment': 'What I have observed as conspicuously minimal in the preaching of evangelical and even reformed Churches is the proclamation of the demands and sanctions of the law of God. To put it bluntly, it is the lack of the enunciation with power, earnestness and passion of the demands and terrors of God's law.'[1]

In this same address on preaching, he went on to show the seriousness of any failure to press the gospel upon all men without distinction: 'If we fail to present this offer with freedom and spontaneity, with passion and urgency, then we are not only doing dishonour to Christ and his glory, but we are also choking those who are the candidates of saving faith.'

The Rev. J. Marcellus Kik shared John Murray's concern for the restoration of *preaching* and he thought that graduates of Westminster Seminary (of which he was a trustee) too often shared in the common failure. This whole subject was discussed between Mr Kik and Iain Murray when the former was in England in 1961, and as a result Mr Kik carried back to John Murray in Philadelphia a proposal that a conference for ministers should be held in 1962, concentrating specifically upon the need for a renewal of

---

[1] *Collected Writings*, vol. 1, pp. 143–51.

preaching. Despite the English venue, it was envisaged that there would be transatlantic support. John Murray was hesitant about speaking at such a conference, for he did not consider himself qualified to give addresses to ministers on the subject of preaching. With characteristic diffidence he wrote to the present writer: 'If some themes or theme were proposed within my competence, then I would heartily consent to take part. Of course, apart altogether from my participation, a week of fellowship with men like Martyn Lloyd-Jones and Jim Grier appeals to me very much. I would be a grateful listener and be ready to participate in discussion.'

When this conference actually met over four days in July 1962 at Leicester in England, Professor Murray gave three addresses, and thereafter the dates of the Leicester Ministers' Conference, as it became known, were never settled without consideration being given to his ability to attend.

At the second Leicester Ministers' Conference, which met for three days in July 1964, John Murray had the responsibility of speaking at five sessions and his contributions, along with memorable sermons by Dr Lloyd-Jones (who was not present in 1962), led to a heightening of expectation in the larger number which assembled the following year. The 1965 Conference met against a background of discussion and concern on the best means to foster unity among evangelical churches amidst a developing ecumenical situation in all the main denominations. Broadly speaking, two viewpoints emerged at that Conference. In both cases their spokesmen were of Calvinistic persuasion; the difference lay rather in policy. In the judgment of some there was a real danger that if a clear-cut Calvinistic doctrinal statement was adopted to promote unity it would have the effect of separating such ministers and congregations from others which, while genuinely evangelical, had still much progress to make in their understanding. They therefore regarded the drawing up of any doctrinal statement as premature and pointed to the need of patience in helping those who, often out of ignorance, were traditionally Arminian.

A second view was that, while it could be conceded that there might be wisdom in proceeding slowly, nevertheless the principle ought to be accepted that there was no hope for a practical, working unity among ministers if the truth or error of Reformed doctrine was permanently left as an open question. It would be sacrificing too much if a broader evangelical unity were to be obtained at the cost of silence on the important differences between Calvinism and Arminianism.

John Murray took this second view and to some extent expounded it in an address to the Conference entitled 'The Creedal Basis of Union in the Church'. He argued that it is the duty of all churches to bear witness to the whole counsel of God; that duty belongs equally to Christians whose understanding of the doctrines of grace must be termed Arminian; and therefore, if such a divergence is to be allowed within and among churches in regular association, it is patently liable to become 'the occasion for disputes that frustrate the unity and dissolve the bond of peace which the church must maintain and display'. 'Though Reformed evangelicals and non-Reformed evangelicals may embrace one another in love, in the bond of fellowship with Christ, and cooperate in many activities that promote the kingdom of God and the interests of Christ's church, yet it is not feasible, and not feasible in terms of commitment to Christ and to the whole counsel of God, to unite in creedal confession as the bond and symbol of ecclesiastical communion.'

The discussion on this subject at the 1965 Conference was all too brief, and it was not helped by the fact that a number of the leading participants scarcely knew one another. Some holding the first view, and closely concerned with conditions in England, were concerned lest there be a doctrinaire commitment to orthodoxy which was over-concerned with the intellectual and the theoretical instead of with the pastoral situation. For the most part those who feared such a drift had not attended the first Leicester Conference, nor did they attend subsequently. John Murray was not unaware of the danger, especially among young men, of an intellectualism which lacked spiritual sensitivity, but the weight of his emphasis fell upon the duty of not abandoning the clear light to which God has brought his church in the creedal confessions drawn up after much scriptural debate in former centuries:

> We must not discount the situation in history in which God has placed us. This would be retrogression. But, of greater moment, it would be dishonouring to the Holy Spirit who in the unfolding events of providence has been enlightening the church to the fuller understanding of His revealed counsel. To go back upon this development and resort to a more attenuated creedal affirmation is to discard the work of the Holy Spirit in the generations of Christian history.[1]

On returning to Badbea from Leicester, Murray wrote to Valerie Knowlton on 13 April 1965:

> I was not so happy about the conference as on other occasions. I was at odds with what appeared to be the prevailing sentiment, but I had the support of some of my best friends, including Iain Murray and others whom I esteem most highly.

Without question the most uplifting session of the 1965 Conference was the one in which Professor Murray brought the proceedings to a close with a sermon on Acts 1:1-2. Through a powerful proclamation of the truth concerning Christ's *continuing* ministry, through the Holy Spirit, on behalf of his church,

---

[1] The substance of Murray's address, here quoted, was printed in *Collected Writings*, vol. 1, pp. 280-7.

attention was turned from our confused discussion on the present situation to great spiritual certainties. The preacher evidently believed that our deliberations had proceeded with far too little regard to the *present* glory of Christ and to the enduement of his Spirit, which is to be expected and prayed for in this age of Pentecost. There has never been a more solemn 'indictment' delivered at the Leicester Conference: the preacher's searching words transcended all differences of policy and came as a rebuke from God for our unspirituality.

Due to a concern that no added strength should be given to existing differences there was no Leicester Conference convened in 1966. It was resumed in 1967 but with no return to discussions on church issues which could best be discussed elsewhere. Emphasis returned to the original purpose of the Conference, namely, to encourage a true revival in the ministry both in doctrine and in experimental piety and godliness. Those who assembled henceforth shared a common conviction that, while we could bear with one another in differences on matters of church order and polity, these fundamentals were the imperative need of the hour. From 1967 John Murray and Jim Grier accepted the joint chairmanship of the Conference, which thereafter met every spring on the understanding that the doctrinal standard upheld by the Conference would be the Calvinistic evangelicalism to which the creeds of the historic Reformed churches were commonly committed. In John Murray's view, the fellowship and co-operation of Presbyterians, Congregationalists, and Baptists of Reformed persuasion, 'on the basis of a common confession and declared objectives without giving up their differences on such questions as government and baptism', was 'an affiliation in the direction of the unity which is demanded of the body of Christ'.

One fear for the Leicester Conference had been that Baptist and Paedobaptist brethren would not remain harmoniously together. The invitation to the 1967 Conference of a younger friend of John Murray's, Pastor A. N. Martin of Essex Fells, New Jersey, was to prove a major influence in preventing any such developments. The two men took different positions on baptism but possessed the highest regard for one another. In a letter to the present writer, John Murray replied in the following terms to an invitation that he should take three evening services at the 1967 conference:

> If Al Martin is to be there I really think he should be asked to take the three evening services you propose for me. He is one of the ablest and most moving preachers I have ever heard. In recent years I have not heard his equal. My memory of preachers goes back sixty years. So, when I say he is one of the ablest, this is an assessment that includes very memorable preachers of the past and present.[1]

This counsel was followed, and with such evidently helpful results that thereafter Al Martin became the most frequent visiting speaker from the United States. John Murray preached at the final session, as in 1965, and that became the established tradition annually until his last attendance in 1971. Murray's attendance at Leicester was of crucial importance in the establishment of an increasingly influential conference. Although initially unknown in person to most who came to Leicester, he became the friend and counsellor of a great many. Those who had only met him once or twice were often amazed at the extent to which he remembered them and their

---

[1] Such was Al Martin's closeness to John Murray that at one Leicester Ministers' Conference he allowed himself the liberty of mimicking the Professor's best-known gesture, the gaze turned downwards to the finger nails of a half-clenched hand, his object being to illustrate in an address on preaching how easily we can fall into the mannerisms of those we esteem. John Murray was chairing that session and sitting with his usual grave countenance, which slowly gave way to a smile!

churches. Affection for him was to become universal among English ministers who knew him. The prejudice entertained by some that Murray was chiefly a dour apologist for Presbyterianism had no place among the growing circle that knew him personally.

It remains to be said, on the subject of John Murray's influence, that it reached its widest scope and most enduring form in his published writings. These consisted, speaking generally, of two kinds of material. First, the shorter magazine articles, already mentioned, which were often compelling reading for Christians with no academic background. Probably his only published book, in this category, is *Redemption: Accomplished and Applied*,[1] the second half of which first appeared as articles in *The Presbyterian Guardian*. Second, there are the volumes that were not intended for popular reading but rather for the aid of serious students. In this group are the books which originated as material in the *Westminster Theological Journal: Christian Baptism*,[2] *Divorce*[3], and *The Imputation of Adam's Sin*.[4] Reviewing the last-named volume in the *Westminster Theological Journal*, Henry J. Knight refers to a section in which 'Murray engages in a type of close reasoning which only an alert mind can follow . . . Here is a book that must be studied, not merely perused. It is a great work of a great theologian.'

More readily followed and yet substantial in content are the two volumes (both originally delivered as lectures), *Principles of Conduct*,[5] which was the first book by Murray to be published in the United Kingdom, and *Calvin on Scripture and Divine Sovereignty*.[6]

In a category of its own, is his *Commentary on the Epistle to the Romans*.[7] In the opinion of Paul Woolley, shared by many, the

---

[1] Eerdmans, 1955, and Banner of Truth, 1961.   [2] OPC, 1952.
[3] OPC, 1953.   [4] Eerdmans, 1959.
[5] Eerdmans and Tyndale Press, 1957.   [6] Presbyterian and Reformed, 1960.
[7] First issued in two volumes, Eerdmans and Marshall, Morgan & Scott, 1959 and 1965.

Commentary on Romans is 'one of the great works of scholarship of all the Christian period'. It is all the more valuable for the fact that its scholarship is not that of the academic theologian, but rather of the school of John Calvin, who wrote of one of his expositions, 'I have faithfully and carefully endeavoured to exclude from it all barren refinements, however plausible and fitted to please the ear, and to preserve genuine simplicity, adapted solidly to edify the children of God.'

Reviewing Volume 1 of Murray's *Romans* in the *Westminster Theological Journal,* William Hendriksen concluded, 'This is exegesis of the highest rank. The book belongs in every minister's library and in the library of every Bible student.' Reviewing Volume 2 in the same journal the late Dr Fred C. Keuhner wrote:

To write a commentary on any book of the Bible is a solemn task. To write one on the Epistle to the Romans is a task both solemn and arduous. And to write one that explains fully and faithfully the profound message of the Apostle in this letter is a labour of love demanding one's highest gifts and deepest devotion . . . Those of us who have had Volume 1 on our shelves since its appearance in 1959 have been waiting expectantly for the publication of Volume 2. We have been looking forward to discovering Murray's treatment of the vexing theological arguments of chapters 9–11 . . . But we must not become surfeited with the exegetical delights of these chapters. There is more to come and to be enjoyed. For when we turn to chapters 12–16 of the epistle we are pleasantly surprised to find that Murray [if this were possible] even surpasses Murray! For nowhere in the commentary does the professor write more lucidly or more pointedly than in those sections of the epistle where Paul sets forth the practical application of the gospel to everyday life. Here the professor of systematic theology becomes the professor of Christian ethics. Here the seminary teacher becomes the counsellor of the

man in the pew. Here he gives the down-to-earth, almost proverbial, advice, 'Few things bring greater reproach upon the Christian
profession than the accumulation of debts and refusal to pay them'
[p. 159]. And again, 'Just as there is to be no social aristocracy in the
church, so there is to be no intellectual autocrat' [p. 137]. And, once
more, 'Pride consists in coveting or exercising a prerogative that
does not belong to us' [p.117]. And, 'The love of God is supreme and
incomparable. We are never asked to love God as we love ourselves
or our neighbour as we love God' [p. 163].

Not many of Murray's writings have as yet been translated.
Those which have appeared in translation include his lecture, *The
Covenant of Grace* (Spanish), *Divorce* (French) and *Redemption:
Accomplished and Applied* (Japanese).

If John Murray erred in anything it was in underestimating the
aid which his written work brought to others. He was slow to
believe that anything he had written justified publication. It is
questionable whether he *offered* anything to publishers, and he was
known to have refused to allow the publication of material which
publishers wished to have. His attitude was characteristically
revealed in 1970 when Al Martin wrote to him to express gratitude
for the great help which his books had proved in his own life and
ministry. To this Murray responded on 26 November 1970:

> I received your letter of the 19th yesterday. It is not possible for me
> to give adequate expression to my appreciation. Furthermore, I have
> been filled with surprise. For I could not have thought that my
> writings could have been to you what you have so kindly stated.
> And that you should have taken the time to write at such length
> adds to my sense of indebtedness to you. So, my friend, thank you.
>
> In all of this we have to realize more and more that God has put
> the treasure in earthen vessels that the excellency of the power may
> be of God and not of us. It is cause for amazement that I should be

in any degree used to contribute to the advance of the gospel. It is all of grace and only exemplifies what is true of salvation in all its aspects and to its utmost reaches, the praise of the glory of God's grace. Eternity will not exhaust our amazement, as it will not exhaust the praise of God's glory in the marvels of redeeming love. Oh, how remiss I am in exploring and appropriating the riches of grace!

10

'The New Work'

APART FROM JOHN MURRAY HIMSELF, no one else in Philadel-phia considered that the termination of his work at West-minster Seminary was desirable in 1964. It was true he had entered upon his sixty-sixth year of life, yet such was his health and sharpness of judgment that his friends could only think of him as being in full maturity.

The fact is, however, that he had looked forward to retirement in the mid-sixties on account of considerations different from those that commonly influence men at this stage in life. It was not that the work of teaching had become a burden, nor that he wished for some repose in the evening of life; it was, primarily, the anticipation he had long entertained of being more fully engaged in preaching and pastoral labour. That, after all, was his first love, and with the passing years his enjoyment of those labours increased rather than diminished.

At first his thought had been that he might be able to serve one of the Canadian churches before ultimately returning to the United Kingdom. There was, however, a second consideration, which now influenced him. In the years after the death of his parents, the family circle at Badbea had been made up of his bachelor brother William, and his two sisters, Johan and Christina. William died in 1963 and it was clear that the maintaining of the croft would soon be too much for the sisters, to whom John was so closely attached. His duty lay at home, and the pull to return and to remain without further delay, was compelling.

It was early in 1964 that he brought to a conclusion the arduous commitment of many years, his *Commentary on Romans*. The large table in the old library, where he had worked 'in season and out of season' for longer than any student of that generation could remember, was now relieved of its accustomed load. In a letter of 3 March 1964, he wrote:

> All my time, apart from lectures and other indispensable commitments, is being devoted to Romans IX–XVI. I have finished the commentary and I have now the introduction and a few appendixes to write. I would like to finish these by the end of March.

Though this goal was reached it was apparent that for another reason the year 1964 could not see the end of his work at Westminster. It had proved impossible to make suitable arrangements to fill the gap which his retirement would cause. The death of his friend, Dr Ned Stonehouse, in 1962, had been a blow to the Seminary, and for the Faculty to lose another of its senior members so shortly after that event was clearly not in the best interests of the work. These considerations were strong enough to lead Professor Murray to agree to the postponement of his retirement. Accordingly, after three months in the United Kingdom in the summer of 1964, when Valerie visited Badbea for the first time, he returned to Westminster in the fall of 1964. It was, however, agreed that he should have an extended leave of absence in 1965, and so by the end of January in that year, he was back at Badbea where he was to remain for the greater part of the next seven months, with Valerie joining his sisters and himself again in August. The ease with which he could revert to outdoor labour at the age of sixty-six was indicative of his physical condition. Notwithstanding a Highland winter, he could report to Valerie on 15 March that he had worked outside every working day except one since his return! On at least one occasion, the Lord's Day also brought unanticipated exertion. On Sunday, 26 February 1965, he had promised to preach at Lairg Free Church for his friend the Rev. John MacLennan. Murray never owned or drove a car in Britain until 1967, and so on this occasion, as on others, he was dependent upon the help of a local driver. The journey to Lairg was uneventful, but as the day progressed, one of the worst snowstorms which he could ever remember came on:

> Coming back from Lairg my driver could not make the brae at Bonar Bridge. So I had to walk from Bonar. I had company, however. The Stewarts who were at their own service in Bonar could not make the brae either and had to walk. I got home all right about 10.15 p.m. I said to my sisters I could have walked another three miles. Less than half a mile from home I had to walk in the field. The snow was too deep on the road.

By this date, although the farm-work at Badbea had been cut down since William's death, there still remained more than enough to occupy him and Laggan, the sheep-dog. There were sixteen sheep and a cow to milk twice a day (a duty which he did for his sisters whenever he was at home). When the Leicester Conference met early in April, and the date for any future conference was discussed, Murray amused the Conference by explaining that this time of year was very difficult for him because it was 'the lambing season'! But for the farmer/theologian it was an entirely serious consideration, and once back at Badbea he was up at 6 a.m. caring for the sheep, which by 29 April had safely given birth to 21 lambs. Such was the labour which he conjoined with the proofreading of his second volume on Romans then nearing its publication!

The present writer has vivid memories of visits to John Murray in this setting. The simplicity of the house seemed in perfect unison with its surroundings. In the parlour there were two or three chairs, a table and a desk, but it was sufficient. Prayer and godliness had long been Badbea's greatest adornment. At the evening meal there was the best of Highland fare for every visitor. This was followed by family worship, begun and closed with prayer, with Psalm and Scripture in between. For the closing prayer all knelt and the throne of God was approached with a reverence borne of long acquaintance with the realities of eternity. It was no mere form. As John wrote to Valerie in March 1965, 'At family worship here we are in 2 Samuel in the morning and Luke at night . . . The Word is living and powerful.'

In the estimation of some hearers, John Murray as a preacher was not always lively and popular. Perhaps the truth is that he was so much accustomed to speaking to candidates for the ministry that possibly he expected too much of the normal type of hearer. In his native Highlands, however, in districts where doctrinal, expository preaching was still prized, he was in his element. 'I like preaching here in my native parish', he wrote to Valerie. The present writer often heard John Murray preach but never with greater liberty than when he was in the North of Scotland. We shall never forget a remarkable sermon which he preached in Clyne Free Church, Brora, Sutherland, in August 1965, where he took the pulpit for the minister, the Rev. John Weir Campbell, who was absent on summer vacation. His text was Acts 2:23: 'Him, being delivered by the determinate counsel and foreknowledge of God, ye have taken, and by wicked hands have crucified and slain: whom God hath raised up, having loosed the pains of death: because it was not possible that he should be holden of it.' The force of the words was unfolded with a spiritual light that was staggering in its effect upon the listeners. The preacher himself was similarly moved. The occasion reminded us of the description Dr Rice of Virginia once gave of a sermon by his friend Archibald Alexander: He appeared 'absolutely overpowered by the truths which he was presenting, and every feature illuminated and glowing with the fire within'.

In September 1965 John Murray was back in Philadelphia for a final fifteen months. There were not a few in the United States who found the thought of his retirement hard to believe. His old colleague R. B. Kuiper, wrote to him on 23 February 1966:

> Dear John,
>
> It was most kind of you to have your publisher send me a complimentary copy of the second volume of your commentary on Romans. I consider the two volumes a masterpiece of believing scholarship.
>
> What do I hear, John? Are you actually going to retire in the near future? But a grandson of mine, a son of Ed and Marietta, will, the Lord willing, be ready to enrol in a seminary in the autumn of 1967, and he is thinking seriously of entering Westminster. What will the poor boy do without you?
>
> Whatever your plans, may God bless you and continue to make you a blessing.
>
> Let me say again what I have said many a time, the best thing I ever did for Westminster was to step aside in 1930, thus making room for John Murray.
>
> Mrs Kuiper sends kindest greetings, as do I.
>
> Cordially yours,
> R. B.

A similar note from Dr Roger Nicole of Gordon Divinity School elicited these paragraphs in Murray's reply:

> Yes, I plan to retire from my work at Westminster at the end of December. I really wanted to do this two years sooner. But the proper arrangements could not be made at Westminster. I plan to return to Scotland. As long as health permits I expect unlimited opportunities in preaching and lecturing. These I wished to take

advantage of years ago. Now I feel I can leave Westminster without any qualms.

Although the actual date from which his retirement was to be effective was 1 January 1967, his departure was to be on 15 December. As the day drew near there were many sad hearts among the student body. Donald McLure, for example, was in his first year at the Seminary. His first memory of Professor Murray stemmed from his childhood when, in William Matheson's congregation at Chesley, to which his parents belonged, the professor from Westminster had conducted a baptismal service during a lightning storm after the electricity supply had failed! As a child McLure preferred Murray's preaching to Matheson's because it was shorter! At sixteen he first talked to Professor Murray about the call to the ministry, but although the latter encouraged him, it was not until he was thirty-three that he came to Westminster. Like other first-year students in 1966 he wished that he had arrived sooner!

Perhaps the only benefit which came to the students through John Murray's retirement was a gift from his library. Many volumes were numbered, pieces of paper bearing these numbers were placed in a hat, and the treasures were bestowed upon the eager recipients according to the number they drew out. The cream of his books, however, went back to Scotland, being done up in eleven-pound[1] parcels with student help. The parcelling of these books does not seem to have been the most proficient of Professor Murray's undertakings, for despite such exclamations as, 'That's a reef-knot, that won't slip!', the books did not complete their journey in the best of shape.

On one of the last occasions when Murray spoke to the students at the Dining Club, he encouraged them to consider the possibility of a particular time in the day being used for prayer for one

---

[1] This was the maximum weight allowed for cheap 'Printed Paper' post.

another, scattered as they soon would be in different parts of the world.

It was not, however, the students who felt his departure most keenly. For his friends on the Faculty, with whom he had been so closely united since the 1930s, the emotion was profound. On the day of parting, Paul Woolley chose to express his thoughts and feelings in a letter, which he sent on to Scotland to be read a week later:

> Westminster Theological Seminary.
> December 15, 1966

Dear John,

Today is one of the saddest days I have experienced in my life. The thought that you will not be a regular and constant part of the Seminary life from now on almost overwhelms me. We have worked together for so many years in a cause that we both love that it brings tears to my eyes to think that you will not be here.

The many years that we worked together as editors of the *Journal* were among the happiest in my life. It was an intense pleasure to work with someone who valued style and taste and accuracy and thought that God's service deserved time and careful attention. You have never been satisfied with second-rate accomplishment in the cause of God's kingdom.

It was a good thing that we did not have an opportunity to say a formal good-bye for it would have been too painful for me. I am not very skilled, as you know, in expressing my thoughts and feelings in speech, and I could not have said what I wanted to. So it is better to remember all the glorious years we have had together and rest in these until God gives us another opportunity to be together either here or in heaven.

I hope the new work you are going to do will be a joy and a delight. It almost seems as though you had accomplished enough for one lifetime, but I know you will never be content not to be about the business of the King of kings. Your commentary on Romans is one of the great works of scholarship of all the Christian period.

Send us good advice from time to time and come back to see us as soon as you possibly can.

Affectionately,
Paul

John Murray left the United States by Cunard line from New York, the port he had first seen forty-three years before. It was to be his last view of the Manhattan skyline, for on his next and final visit to the States, in 1969, the journey was made by air. Far more important to him, though he did not know it at the time: the moments before sailing were the last spent with Edward J. Young, who was only to live another fourteen months. In a letter to his older friend on 18 February 1967, Dr Young wrote:

Dear John,

It is now just over two months ago that we said 'good-bye' to you on the ship at New York. We have had two months of wintry weather with several heavy snowstorms. It was snowing heavily this morning, but the sun came out and the day has been quite lovely.

We do miss you here, John. I want to take this means to tell you how grateful I am to you for all that you have done for me. It is difficult to believe that an association of thirty years is now at an end, and I know that I shall greatly miss your help and wisdom.

I am particularly grateful that you have instilled in me a love for the Scriptures and an understanding of the importance of Systematic Theology. I remember that when I was a student and you had lectured on Romans 5:12–19, I was so moved by the content of those verses that I took a long walk that afternoon just to think about them. It is going to be difficult carrying on without you.

Thank you, John, for all you have done. I realize how inadequate words are, but I do want to assure you of my gratitude and appreciation. May God give you many more fruitful years for His service, if it be His will.

Please don't bother to answer this note. We all miss you but will keep you in our prayers that God will keep you in good health and continue to use you.

Sincerely,
Joe

P. S. And thank you too for conducting the course in Old Testament Biblical Theology.

Quietness had fallen upon the home to which John Murray returned, for his sister Johan had died only the week before he left Westminster, and now only Christina remained. As he read the above letters from long-beloved colleagues in the solitude of the Scottish Highlands, we do not doubt that his customary composure was greatly strained. And it would be no less so in February 1968, when a telegram bore the grievous news of Joe Young's heart attack and sudden death. Reflecting on the latter event he was to write: 'In the last few years before retirement from my work at the Seminary, I was deeply impressed by the evidence my friend gave of the maturing fruit of the Spirit. But little did I think that he was being rapidly prepared for the immediate presence of the Saviour . . .'

When Paul Woolley spoke of John Murray's return to the United Kingdom as an entrance to 'new work' he was undoubtedly reflecting his friend's own view. Others thought the same. In an editorial tribute, entitled 'Beloved Professor', in the December 1966, *Presbyterian Guardian,* Robert E. Nicholas commented, 'It would not surprise us too much should we hear ere long that he has become an undershepherd for some flock of the Lord's redeemed.' In the seven months' leave in 1965, which had included

visits to Holland and Northern Ireland, there had been almost as
many preaching engagements offered to him in Scotland as he
could undertake, and various parties in England were now also
pressing for his help. Opportunities for serving the gospel in
Britain were thus more plentiful for him than they had ever been
before, and, as he reported to the presbytery of New York and New
England (of which he remained a member), these opportunities
were deeply prized. There was, in addition, his hope of doing some
further writing. In 1966 he had undertaken a commitment to
prepare six entries on doctrinal themes for the Zondervan *Pictorial
Encyclopedia of the Bible,* and when these were completed he had
thoughts of writing on sanctification, a subject which deeply interested him, or perhaps on aspects of eschatology.

But before he could truly settle to this new stage of life in
Britain there was one outstanding matter to be settled. In Philadelphia he had left Valerie Knowlton, now the holder of a Harvard
doctorate and Assistant Professor of Anatomy at the Woman's
Medical College of Pennsylvania, but their regular letters, maintained for twelve years whenever they were away from each other,
had long become insufficient. Even at Badbea, life without Valerie
could not be contemplated, and thus at last, in the autumn of 1967,
their friends heard the long-expected news that the wedding was
to be at the Hall of the Free Church of Scotland, Migdale, Bonar
Bridge, on 7 December with a reception following at the Bridge
Hotel. In their joy at the event none asked why it had not come
about earlier. In any case, as John Murray half-smilingly revealed,
sixty-nine was no family record for a first marriage. 'If I marry in
the next year', he was heard to say on the Westminster Campus in
1966, 'I will be younger than my grandfather was at his marriage!'

Still greater was the joy when, as 1968 ran its course, the news
circulated that, after more than sixty years, the birth of a baby was
again expected in Badbea! About the time the birth was expected

'The New Work'

John Murray had promised to preach to the Free Church congregation at Tain where the minister, the Rev. Clement Graham, was laid aside by illness. When the day came to fulfil the engagement, Sunday, 22 December, Mrs Murray was some forty miles away in hospital in Inverness. Returning to Mr Graham's manse after the morning service, John Murray had commenced lunch with the family when a messenger arrived, and he was summoned to the privacy of another room. In a few minutes he was back at the dinner table. With half a smile and a mannerism well-known to his acquaintances, he informed the company, 'Well, you know, I have a son!' The next day he carried out his first new duty and wrote the following:

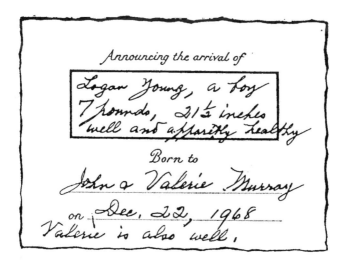

Announcing the arrival of
Logan Young, a boy,
7 pounds, 21½ inches
well and apparently healthy
Born to
John & Valerie Murray
on Dec, 22, 1968
Valerie is also well,

As already indicated, Logan's birth was on a Sunday, and if Mr Murray was to see his wife and child that day and take evening service in Tain, it would mean a tiring drive to Inverness and back. Mr Graham therefore pressed his visitor to allow someone else to take his place in the second service. The suggestion brought a swift and characteristic response: 'No, it's on condition that I would be back here in time for the evening service that I agreed to go to the hospital. Nothing short of a breakdown in health would justify a man in breaking a commitment to preach!'

With Logan's arrival, John Murray's work began to undergo something of a revolution. It was no longer possible for Mrs Murray to accompany him away from home, as she did for three weeks in England in September 1968, and his presence was increasingly needed at Badbea. Their last period away was to be to the States with Logan late in 1969, when John Murray spoke at the Seminary for the last time. Before that visit Murray wrote to the clerk of the Orthodox Presbyterian Church Presbytery of New York and New England, regretting that he could not be present in time for their meeting on 14 October, and requesting leave to be permitted to labour outside the bounds of presbytery. In replying to him, the Presbytery Clerk confirmed that his request was granted and added: 'We were pleased that if you could not attend Presbytery here in October, it was at least in part due to the "family responsibilities" mentioned in your letter. We rejoice in your family responsibilities . . .' This gladness, it might be added, was universal among all who knew John and Valerie Murray.

There was, by 1969, another factor which was to limit Professor Murray's movements. His sister Christina was now suffering from a disability that sometimes accompanies advancing years. Her mind, once bright and sharp, had grown weary, and though spiritual realities and the memories of earlier times remained undimmed, she was losing contact with day-to-day responsibilities. The work she had once sweetly undertaken now stood still, and, more seriously, she could not be depended upon to take care of herself if left alone. The friends of recent years, including Valerie Murray, she scarcely knew at all, and it therefore fell to John to exercise a ministry of care and of constant watchfulness.

For as long as possible, Professor Murray sought to maintain his wider, speaking ministry along with these family duties. In particular it should be mentioned how often his help was sought by many of the Christian Unions in Scottish universities of which even the nearest was a considerable journey from Badbea. The visits to universities, which he made at this period, are well remembered today. One former Aberdeen theological student, now a Church of Scotland minister, expressed the opinion that 'an unforgettable lecture on the Atonement by Professor Murray was worth a term of the lectures we were accustomed to'. On another occasion, at the Christian Union of the same University, 'John Murray weaved his way, without note and with his Greek Testament closed, through Romans 5:12–21, parenthesis and all, in an amazing way!'

His last visit to the Leicester Conference came in 1971. It involved some two days' travelling there and back, and he was only able to reach Leicester, in the English Midlands, on the day before the Conference ended. Immediately on arriving he gave an address on 'The Sabbath' and, once more, he took the final session of the Conference, preaching from John 6:37. Such was his commitment to what the Leicester Conference stood for that he thought no effort too great if it would encourage the brethren.

Three months later the Murrays' second child, Anne-Margaret, was born safely on 21 July 1971.[1] From about this time Professor Murray found it impossible to be away from home overnight, and consequently the number of engagements which he could henceforth accept became restricted to the comparatively few congregations which were to be found within thirty or forty miles of his home. The family was his care and delight and everything necessary to the needs of an infant's world he was quick to learn.

[1] Anne-Margaret, a sweet and beautiful child, was never strong. She died on 5 January 1976.

'John', as Valerie was later to recall, 'was a very excellent father and he was thrilled to have the children.' He deviated from the traditional Highland custom in his belief that infants should go to church as early as possible. Logan at two-and-a-half was well established in that routine by the time Valerie had to discontinue her attendance for a period at the time of Anne-Margaret's birth. Logan was no problem if he could sit and sleep beside his father in the pew, but frequently Professor Murray was supplying the pulpit of a local congregation twice each Lord's Day, and the only solution was for Logan to be in the pulpit with his father, where he slept quietly on the floor during the sermon. John Murray's customary fondness for walking up and down in the expansive pulpits of the Highlands while preaching was thus for some months curtailed by his fear of stepping on Logan! The fact that his dark suit was often inevitably covered with white fluff transferred from Logan's clothing before the service, troubled him far less than if Logan had not been there at all!

Logan spent much of his time in his father's presence. The few memories which he was to retain of his father in later years concerned their daily walks, digging together in the garden, and the learning of Psalms.

Apart from correspondence, little writing was now done, and Professor Murray's thought that he might re-work some of his lectures for publication was not fulfilled. Had there been time for original writing, the following scrap, found among his papers after his death, suggests what new line he might have pursued!

1. Who made you? God.
2. What else did God make? God made all things.
3. Why did God make all things? For his own glory.
4. Will all things glorify him? Yes, all his works will praise him.
5. Who was the first man God made? Adam.
6. " " " " woman " " ? Eve.

7. Did Adam have a daddy? No, God made him from the dust of the ground and breathed life into him.
8. Did Eve have a daddy? No, God made her from one of Adam's ribs.
9. Were Adam and Eve good when God made them? Yes, very good.
10. Did they continue good? No.
11. Why not? They sinned by disobeying God.
12. What was this sin? They ate forbidden fruit.
13.

It troubled him that there was so little good literature suitable for children and he could not accept the idea that, with a modicum of Scripture, a child's reading diet can be supplemented by fiction. He was equally troubled that in the Scottish Highlands, where Christian education had once been so universal, there appeared to be a general readiness to commit children from Christian homes to schools where the authority of the biblical revelation was not recognized. On this subject he gave a masterly address in Dornoch in 1972, and another in Dingwall in 1973.[1] One practical result of this concern was the formation of a committee of like-minded Christians, in which he worked tirelessly, and a small Christian primary school was started in Dornoch. It was here that Logan began his schooling and until February of 1975 John Murray would daily drive his son into Dornoch, where he waited to return with him at lunchtime.

One form of service which was not given up even after his activities were restricted to the area of Bonar Bridge was the counselling which he had undertaken for many years. Of course, this

---

[1] *Collected Writings*, vol. 1, pp. 367–74. Faced once with the question, 'How do you account for the spiritual decline in Scotland?', he commenced his answer with the words, 'The surrender of education of the young by parents to the State. This had not been so in former years.'

was now generally carried on by means of correspondence, but not invariably. It was not unknown for ministers to phone from the United States asking for advice. One minister who went to Dr Van Til with a particularly difficult problem was told: 'Get in touch with John Murray. He understands and knows how to apply Scripture better than I do. A long phone call to Badbea resulted, and when the enquirer acted upon the advice he received, it proved to be right.

John Murray was a regular adviser of the Banner of Truth Trust long before he formally became a trustee in 1971. There was a regular flow of correspondence on the subject of future publications. The following extract from a letter of 3 December 1973, to the present writer, is typical:

> On Commentaries proposed for publication I do not have access at present to Plummer on Psalms and so I cannot give a judgment. Horne on Psalms I do not know. I share your own doubt regarding Alexander and for the reasons you mention. I would highly recommend Calvin but not the three-volume edition. The five-volume set may for that reason be prohibitive, however.
>
> I am somewhat disappointed with Hutcheson on John, on the ground of exegesis, not on the ground of devotional or theological value. If Fergusson on the Epistles is similar I have my questions.
>
> An edition of the Westminster Confession with Catechisms and Directory etc., appeals to me greatly. The F.P. edition has done well on remedying errors in the text of the Confession. But a demy-size edition is most desirable.
>
> I long for a good edition of *The Pilgrim's Progress*. I accept your proposal respecting edition. I have nothing else to propose.
>
> I know nothing of Phelps or Nettleton. So I defer to those who do.
>
> I disagree with E. J. Young on at least one point of exegesis in *Isaiah 53*. But this does not affect its merit as a whole.
>
> Go ahead with J. W. Alexander: *Thoughts on Preaching*.

Books by seven of the authors mentioned in this letter were subsequently published by the Trust.

Counsel given to the Trust was by no means confined to books. One vexed question being discussed in Reformed circles at this date was the theology of revivals. Some Calvinistic circles, with which Westminster Seminary was occasionally identified, took the position that, as the Spirit was 'poured out' once at Pentecost, no future occurrences of that event should be anticipated. According to this view, the fullness and baptism with the Spirit is given to all Christians at their regeneration and therefore 'revivals' must not be thought of as larger givings of the Spirit to the church. Those who took a contrary position, however, sought to show that both Scripture and church history warranted prayer for a further giving of the Spirit, and that larger measures of his grace and power were to be sought for the advancement of Christ's kingdom. Patently not all Christians are in the experimental condition of assurance and praise exemplified in the *Acts of the Apostles*. With his unusual discrimination John Murray saw that there were two lines of scriptural truths in this debate, truths which ought to complement one another and not serve to polarize two parties. There is both the *uniqueness* of Pentecost as in Acts chapter two, and the *continuing* need to seek for 'copious manifestations of the Holy Spirit's power and grace'.

When we asked Professor Murray's judgment on an article from our pen on 'Baptism with the Spirit: What is the Scriptural Meaning?', intended for the *Banner of Truth* magazine, the main part of his response, written on 19 February 1974, was as follows:

> On page 7 the sentence I have marked would need greater discrimination. Acts 2:38 speaks of 'the gift of the Holy Spirit' and I think the charismatic gift is *particularly* in view in that passage. I agree with your thought. But I think the formulation should be modified

in respect of Acts 2:38. On page 10 the sentence I have marked seems to me to require more perspicuity. But perhaps it does not. On the same page, what I have marked certainly needs some expansion to make your point clear.

I think you have made out a strong case for the position you are propounding, and some of your criticisms levelled against the other viewpoint are exceedingly cogent. I agree entirely with your contention on the need for more emphasis upon the work of the Holy Spirit and for the appreciation of the fact that since Pentecost this is the age of the Holy Spirit. I believe we have done great dishonour to the Holy Spirit in these regards and that our poverty springs to a large extent from this dishonour. I agree also with your main contention that there are seasons of great refreshing from the presence of the Lord (cf. *Acts* 3:19) and that we should earnestly pray for and expect these as increased and copious manifestations of the Holy Spirit's power and grace. Examples of these are the Protestant Reformation and the 'revivals' you so appropriately refer to, as well as other most remarkable movements not mentioned by you. I could go on in this vein. But it is not necessary. I simply voice my agreement with you and the worthies of the past to whom you appeal.

This brings me, however, to what may be my main point by way of critique. It concerns what you yourself say in the last paragraph of page 13 in the sentence beginning: 'It is a serious injustice'. I personally have hesitation in using the terminology frequently employed and for which you contend with forceful argumentation. But I am in entire agreement with the viewpoint behind the terminology. Now although there is the admission in the paragraph to which I referred, your polemic as a whole is directed to another impression and I think that is unfortunate. So much emphasis falls on terminology that I get the *impression* that those not employing it are really opposed to the thesis itself. At least, I as one not constrained to certain terms, would take umbrage from the article on the ground that I was being misrepresented.

I do not think that enough has been said in your article on the epochal significance of Pentecost as a pivotal *event* in the history of redemption.[1]

One of John Murray's greatest joys in what were to be the last years of his life was his regular pastoral oversight of the Free Church at Ardgay, a congregation some two miles from Badbea, and just south of Bonar Bridge. He had frequently helped in this vacant charge, where faithful missionaries had kept the work going, but in March 1972, Clement Graham, on behalf of the Free Church Presbytery of Tain, had formally asked him if he could undertake the week-by-week care of the congregation. Ardgay's last missionary had died suddenly, and the denomination was not in a position to replace him. John Murray responded immediately to Mr Graham's invitation and from that time forward, except for the first Sabbath of the month (when he supplied the Croick Free Church) or for an occasional visit to another church, he was virtually the pastor of the Ardgay congregation, preaching twice every Sunday to perhaps two dozen people and visiting amongst them during the week. This he enjoyed immensely, and it added to his happiness that Logan, too, with the interest of a child, began to look forward to the services at Ardgay.

He seemed, in his preaching at Ardgay, to return often to the vision of God the Father, and sometimes, as he sought to trace the entire work of salvation to this glorious source, he rose to heights where he could not easily be followed. In the last few Sundays of

---

[1] The article was subsequently printed in the April 1974 issue of the magazine. The paragraph to which Professor Murray refers on p. 13 of the original manuscript occurs on p. 19. The above was only one of many instances in which we benefited from his careful criticism.

his pulpit work, however, the sermons reverted to the simpler homily such as his father would have preached. At the end of the services on 1 February 1975, he told his congregation that he would have to discontinue preaching for a while. Following a medical examination it was decided that he should enter the hospital at Golspie, Sutherland, on 10 February. Before he did so he sat once more with the Rev. Malcolm MacDonald in the Free Church Manse at Creich, and in the course of conversation he confided to his friend: 'I am an old man and I have had many a good day. Such was the energy I used in former years that I did not expect to live to be old.' He was to make a similar remark to his wife in commenting on God's goodness in sparing him so long, mentioning, in particular, the hard work in which he had engaged in New England.

Even though he had visibly lost weight it was not easy for his friends to think of him as elderly. Until near the end of 1974 his vigour seemed undiminished, and they knew nothing of the pain and excessive weariness which had suddenly come upon him. Once in hospital, it was confirmed that he was suffering from cancer, that the end might be soon, and that there was nothing that medical science could do. When the present writer heard this news from the sufferer himself as he sat in his hospital bed it scarcely seemed possible. His face was not then wasted by illness, and only a few weeks previously he had been writing letters to me in his usual firm hand respecting matters of mutual concern in the work of the Banner of Truth Trust.

My mind was numbed and focused upon his condition, but his was as alert as ever, and he wished to speak about matters to which I found it hard to give my attention. As we parted he expressed the hope that he might yet have a little strength given to him to lengthen his days. Though he did not say so, I knew he wished it for the sake of the three who had been God's gift to him in those relationships which are uniquely precious.

'The New Work'

He returned home from hospital early in March and he had no thought of being confined to bed. He walked about freely and his bearing gave friends who visited him the hope that they would hear him preach again. But secretly he suffered constant pain, at times intense, and this, combined with an inability to eat, was to bring all his native strength to an end. When too tired for company he would go to his bedroom and there often repeat Psalms to himself, or else he would sit on the steps of the bungalow looking out upon that scene which had not changed since he knew it as a child. Among the letters that came to him at this period was one from Cornelius Van Til:

March 6, 1975

Dear John,

Yesterday Paul Woolley called up to say that in a letter to him you said that you wished to be remembered to us. That did our hearts good. We had already learned about your illness. So I was, in any case, going to write to you and tell you how much you have meant to me.

You will not remember, but when you were about to leave us and return to your home-land we shook hands. I turned away and wept.

Throughout the years of our association together you were to me (a) an example of godly living and (b) of utter devotion to your Lord. It was obvious to all of us that you loved your Saviour passionately, that you sought to serve your Lord with utter sincerity, and that your ambition was to point out to all men everywhere that only by the 'good pleasure' of God can they be saved from the wrath of God. Nothing has helped me more, John, than to hear you pour out your heart in prayer for the church of Jesus Christ as a whole and for individuals in particular.

Ed Clowney remarked to several of us in the Faculty room, the other day, how his heart had been stirred when you led in prayer at the occasion of his mother's death.

I recall that my father remarked about the genuine communion of saints that he had experienced when, visiting him, you had led him, together with yourself, to the throne of grace.

Many a time, in chapel, and in Faculty meetings, I was personally brought closer to my Saviour by your prayer.

As I write I think of Dr Machen, lying on his death-bed in Bismarck, North Dakota, sending you a telegram: 'How wonderful is the active obedience of Christ!' You had helped him see the significance of this aspect of his Saviour's work as he had never seen it before.

And then I think of one occasion when you rebuked me for some folly of mine. I fully deserved it but you alone had the courage to administer the admonishment of Christ to me.

But I shall not continue. Allow me only to mention your love for the Psalms of David. Rena and I were brought up on the Psalms. We still sing them together. When she underwent surgery recently we sang them together in the hospital. She sang one of them as she came out of the state of unconsciousness . . .

And now, John, may the Lord bless thee and keep thee, cause his face to shine upon thee and be gracious unto thee; may he lift up his countenance upon thee and give thee peace.

Hattie de Waard,
Rena and Kees Van Til

By early April John was so weak that the thoughts of those around him turned more steadily to the surer expectation of a brighter world than this.

Mrs Elizabeth Tallach, whose parents had known and loved him in his youth, and whose own friendship with him went back over many years, writes of the last visit she paid to Badbea some four weeks before his death:

On arrival I was welcomed by Mrs Murray and their two lovely children. Shortly afterwards Mr Murray joined us. He looked very reduced and tired, but warmly welcoming. While Mrs Murray prepared a cup of tea, I remarked to J.M. that in the morning I had been thinking of the words, 'Unto us a child is born, unto us a Son is given.' 'Oh, yes', he said eagerly, 'here you have the two natures of Christ, the Son from everlasting given, and the Child born in time. I also think that "wonderful" should be an adjective, and that the passage should read, Wonderful Counsellor. But however it may be understood, He is the Counsellor, and He is wonderful.' He went on to speak of the 'Everlasting Father', and how this title did not in any way interfere with the special relationship of the Father in the Godhead, but referred to Christ's kingly office, ruling over His kingdom. It would have been worth while to travel to Badbea, even to hear J.M.'s asking of a blessing on the tea now prepared, and his earnest pleading that fellowship in Christ and the Gospel be cemented more and more. After tea, he led in singing the first four verses of Psalm 40, in a clear voice and melodious, beginning,

I waited for the Lord my God
and patiently did bear;
At length to me he did incline
my voice and cry to hear.

As I rose to go, J.M. said, 'I often go back in thought to happy days I spent in 'Timaru', Strathpeffer, with your father and mother and Uncle Donald and all of you. It was Bethel.' I ventured to say that that fellowship would yet be resumed without interruption or end, and he smiled brightly.

Most people who visited Professor Murray during his last, very testing illness were impressed by his calmness of spirit, and what appeared like complete absence of self-pity. 'Strong in faith, giving glory to God.'

On 14 April, as Malcolm MacDonald was leaving after a visit, John Murray spoke to him very deliberately about the possibility of his own early death and, requesting that the burial service be taken at the Creich church, he gave precise instructions on the funeral arrangements which he wished. Three days later, David Freeman, his early friend of Princeton days, found him weak but as keen as ever in thought. Pulling out of his pocket a New Testament in the New International Version translation he asked Freeman his opinion on it. 'For use in worship', his friend replied, 'it does not, in my view, take precedence over the Authorized Version.' John Murray expressed agreement and yet went on to say that he liked this version. The subsequent discussion revealed how closely he had read it. Among its defects he noted the rendering 'only Son' for 'only begotten Son'. He was decisive that the latter was superior and that 'only Son' takes away something. Again, he would not consent to 'flesh' being rendered 'sinful flesh'. After their conversation David Freeman wondered, as he had done before, at John's comprehensive understanding of Scripture.

As April passed and May came, his sufferings were intense. Archibald Alexander of Princeton has wisely remarked on the reasons why, as death approaches, the conscious enjoyment of Christ may vary so greatly among Christians: 'The difference between the comforts of dying saints may be attributed, first, to divine sovereignty, which distributes grace and consolation as seemeth good unto Him; secondly, to bodily temperament, some persons being more fearful than others, and more prone to suspect their own sincerity; and thirdly, to the nature of the disease by which the body is brought down to the grave . . .'[1] In the case of this servant of Christ the degree of pain was great. His experience

---

[1] Archibald Alexander, *Thoughts on Religious Experience* (1844; repr. London: Banner of Truth, 1967), p. 241.

was like that of a Puritan divine who exclaimed, 'Hold out, faith and patience!' And like the Psalmist's, who cried, 'Save me, O God; for the waters are come in unto my soul!'

After a long and sleepless night, he sat up in bed at 7 a.m. on the morning of 8 May and asked for his medicine. Then, with one sentence of prayer, he committed the family to the care of God, after which with that note of kindly authority which was with him to the end, he bade his wife, and his sister who was present, to go and rest.

About an hour later he passed through his last conflict with pain and in that conflict threw himself upon the comprehensive petition which has been the final prayer of many children of God, 'God be merciful to me a sinner.' Thereafter he lapsed into a coma until about half an hour after twelve noon when he fell asleep in Jesus.

We do not know how many copies of the Greek New Testament John Murray wore out—he left several in that condition among his books. But in the last one which he used he had written inside the covers in the closing weeks of his life:

O Lord, all that I do desire
is still before thine eye,
And of my heart the secret groans
not hidden are from thee.

Now his desires were satisfied and his spirit was filled, as it could not be on earth, 'with holy and adoring amazement at the condescensions of trinitarian love and grace'.

The funeral, which took place on Tuesday, 13 May is described by the Rev. Kenneth J. MacLeay of Beauly:

The Kyles of Sutherland were enveloped in mist, and the day damp and cold; as though in sympathy with the many mourners who gathered at Bonar Bridge from North, South, East and West, yea, and from across the Atlantic, to pay their last respects to the memory of Professor John Murray. Between four and five hundred people were congregated there in the historic Free Church, Creich, the Church of the revered Dr Aird, for the funeral service of this saintly scholar.

The impressive silence which pervaded this large representative company of ministers from all denominations, and people from all walks in life, indicated their consciousness that a Prince in Israel had fallen. The service was conducted by Rev. M. MacDonald, minister of the Creich congregation, assisted by Dr Freeman, USA, Rev. John MacSween, Point, Isle of Lewis, Rev. D. Lamont, Edinburgh, and Rev. Hector Cameron, Dornoch, the Praise being led by Mr Hector MacLeod, Bonar Bridge. The dignity, coupled with the simplicity of this service, in true Reformation style, was just as John Murray would have desired. He had gone forth from this small scattered community to become one of the world's leading theologians. Both in America and this country he influenced many young ministers of the Gospel, confirming them in the faith of the Reformation. Having finished his course, having kept the faith, it now seemed fitting that the small cemetery on the shores of the Kyles of Sutherland should contain the remains of this worthy servant of Christ until the day break and the shadows flee away.

* * * * *

Various tributes were written after John Murray's death and we must confine ourselves to extracts from three.

Cornelius Van Til wrote:

John Murray I held in high esteem as a Christian, as a personal friend and as a colleague for many years.

As to his character there was, first, his deep *humility* before God, and even before men who were with him, as he knew, seeking to serve their Master.

There was, second, his *boldness*. He feared God and therefore feared no man. His reputation as a scholar was never of primary concern to him, so long as by his work, the triune God of Scripture was magnified. In both of these respects he resembled Dr Machen and Dr Vos.

Humble boldness marked John's every doing, no less when he was known throughout the world as the greatest living Calvin scholar than when he first began his career of teaching as an instructor at Princeton.

There was, third, *his faithfulness*, faithfulness toward God and then toward men. Back in 1929 John promised Caspar Wistar Hodge that he would teach under him as an instructor for a year even after the split. This was a promise to a man, but for John a promise to a man is first of all a promise to God . . .

John was of inestimable value to Westminster Seminary, equally to its students and to its Faculty. He was the 'conscience' of all of us. Blessed be his memory!

Allan A. MacRae, whose friendship with the subject of this volume commenced in their days together at Princeton, concluded his memories already quoted in these pages, with the words:

John, with his one eye, did more reading and study than most Christian workers do with two eyes. His life presents a picture of loyalty to Christ and to the Scripture, of kindly interest in all other human beings, particularly those of the household of faith, and of energetic tireless activity to make his beliefs known. His example should encourage every one of us as we seek to emulate his faithfulness and his industry.

Finally, the words of John R. de Witt:

We shall miss him immensely. He was a good and gracious man in every way, a man of humble, child-like faith and piety. He was also one of the best modern representatives of the old Reformed School of theology. We shall not see his like again. His own cast of mind was conservative and he was a Highlander through and through. But at the same time he was altogether catholic in his sympathies and not in the least narrow, bigoted or closed. To know him was to understand in a measure what the great divines of the 16th and 17th centuries must have been like.

Appendix:
Answers to Queries[1]

Westminster Seminary,
Philadelphia
PA 19118
14 Dec. 1963[2]

Dear Mr Green,

Thank you very much for both of your letters and for your kind remarks. It is most generous of you to have sent through your bank the gift for the Seminary. You will receive acknowledgement and thanks in due time from the executive secretary. I have asked that Bulletins be sent to you regularly. There is no charge for these.

I have asked the Secretary in charge of *Journal* distribution to send you the back issues for 1963 and 1964 and forthcoming issues for 1965. For these three years the charge is $3.00. The policy of the editors is not to give free copies of the *Journal*. So I am sorry to have to tell you that you will be billed for $3.00. But this is, of course, what you asked for in your letter.

---

[1] In the 1960s and early 1970s Professor Murray corresponded regularly with Mr Jack Green of Pontefract, Yorkshire, often in response to queries Mr Green had raised. A series of these letters is included here.

[2] Though dated as shown, the postmark on this letter reads 16 Dec. 1964. The contents of the letter seem to confirm that 1964, not 1963, was intended.

Shall I hope to see you at Leicester on 5 April? It would be a great joy to meet you there. I leave again for Scotland, around 25 January, the Lord willing.

With warm regards
I am
Cordially Yours
John Murray

JOHN 3:16

Westminster Seminary,
20 Nov. 1965

Dear Mr Green,

How good it was to have your letter of the 10th inst. and to have news of you. I was in Europe 7½ months but our paths did not cross. Of course, I spent most of the time in Scotland and my trips to and through England were all by plane. I must have flown over or near Pontefract a few times.

I can fully appreciate your difficulty with John 3:16.

1. It is well to appreciate fully the design stated in 16b and the certainty and security it enunciates – the infallible salvation of all who believe. Now the salvation spoken of in vs. 17 cannot have less security and efficacy in view of the close interdependence of the two verses. But if so, 'the world' cannot refer to 'all men' unless all men are ultimately saved, an unscriptural position.

2. We must appreciate the particular emphasis of each text. A text cannot reflect on every aspect of truth. The accent in 16a falls on *what* God loved, not on how many, on what God loved in respect of its quality, mankind lost; cursed by sin, detestable, the contradiction of God and of what he is. That brings out the marvel and greatness of God's love, and the intensity is expressed in whom he gave unto the end of making salvation secure and certain. Now

nothing less than God's love on the highest level can measure up to this love (cf. *Eph.* 2:5; *Rom.* 8:29, 32, 39). But the point is that in this text the whole emphasis falls on the *character* of that which God loved.

3. We shall have to restrict the word 'world' to mankind, for to mankind alone is 16b relevant. The same must apply to 17. I do not think it is necessary or warranted to take these verses as referring to the territorial globe or the heavens after the pattern of *Rom.* 8:17–23; *2 Pet.* 3:13 *et al.* Again each text has its own denotative scope and universe of discourse.

> With warmest regards, I am,
> Cordially Yours,
> John Murray

SINLESSNESS OF CHRIST

> Badbea,
> 22 Dec. 1967

Dear Mr Green,

Thank you for your kind letter of 29 Nov. 1967. I am deeply interested in your thoughts regarding theological training. May you be directed and sustained and rough places made smooth in the fulfilment of the Lord's will.

I am not sure that copies of the series 'Substitutes', etc. are still available except in bound issues of the *Presbyterian Guardian*. Bound issues would be quite expensive.

I think we should maintain Christ's impeccability. In my view this in no way interferes with the reality and poignancy of his temptations. It was his impeccable holiness that added intensity to the grief of temptation. For the holier a person is, the more excruciating is encounter with solicitation to the opposite. Even in the case of believers, the more sanctified a person is, and, for that reason, the less the ability to succumb, the greater is the pain of being tempted.

In other words, the greater is the sense of the iniquity and vileness of sin, the greater is the poignancy of solicitation to commit the same. In the case of our Lord this is true to an incomparable degree because he was perfect. Furthermore, the impeccability in no way detracts from the comfort for the believer. For example, from whom among the saints do we derive the greatest support and strength in our temptations? Is it not from the more mature and sanctified who are able to resist and overcome rather than from the weak and erring who are so frequently the victims of temptation? So again this is true supremely and incomparably in what is contemplated in Hebrews 4:15.

May I add another consideration that may help? A believer cannot commit the unpardonable sin; he cannot apostatize from the faith. But this aspect of 'impeccability' does not eliminate temptation thereanent.

With these thoughts I close and extend to you warm greetings for 1968.

I am,
Cordially Yours,
John Murray

WOMEN TEACHING IN THE CHURCH

Badbea,
10 Jan. 1969

My Dear Friend,

It is good of you to write and do so with such kindness. I may not be able to answer your questions satisfactorily and certainly not with the detail they merit.

1. I believe *1 Cor.* 14:33–40; *1 Tim.* 2:11–15 are decisive against the teaching or preaching ministry in the church on the part of women. Paul appeals to these considerations: (a) the uniform practice of the

churches ('as in all the churches of the saints') [1 Cor. 14:33]; (b) the requirement of the law [1 Cor. 14:34]; (c) the order established in creation [1 Tim. 2:13]. Hence the shame of violating the prohibition [1 Cor. 14:35]. Now as to leading in prayer I believe there are two considerations in support of a similar silence on the woman's part. (a) The 'silence' enjoined in the above passages creates a strong presumption against audible prayer. (b) In 1 Tim. 2:8 'the men' are distinctly specified as those who are to pray where the praying is obviously that of a public character. Our version may not adequately bring this out. It is not simply men but 'the men' and then not mankind generically but men as distinguished from women (τους ἀνδρας). This seems to me confirmed by verse 9; for then Paul proceeds to give the injunction appropriate to women: 'In like manner I will that women', etc. If women were likewise in view in verse 8, it must be strange that the behaviour enjoined upon women would be of such a different character and the change so abruptly introduced.

2. Respecting 1 Cor. 11:2–16 a great deal of nonsense has been written to promote the notion that the provisions were applicable to a local situation and therefore not relevant to the church universally and permanently. In refutation there are these observations. (a) The apostle appeals to the order of creation as that which demands covering for the woman (vss. 8–12). This order is permanently relevant. (b) The man is the image and glory of God (vs. 7): this must be always recognized and the authority it involves exercised. Hence the covering as the sign of subjection on the part of the woman. It is not the particularly oppressive behaviour of the Corinthian women that makes the covering necessary, though this would accentuate the necessity, but the position of the woman in the divinely instituted economy. (c) Nature teaches the practice (vss. 14, 15). What this refers to I do not venture to say. But it must refer to something in the nature of things. (d) Verse 10 means, I think, that

the woman has the sign of subjection. They [the angels?] are so attuned to God's will and so sensitive to propriety that they could not but be shocked by the impropriety in view. Regard for the angels dictates the sign of subjection. Could we conceive of this reference to the angels as having only local or temporary relevance? (e) Verse 16, in a way somewhat similar to *1 Cor.* 14:33, extends the perspective beyond the local situation. All of these points could be expanded. But they are indicative of the abiding relevance of the requirement placed upon women at Corinth. No doubt there were peculiar conditions at Corinth that made urgent the need for the apostolic injunctions. But a great deal of the New Testament is occasioned by the need of giving direction in a particular situation. This is signally true of the second half of this chapter (vss. 17–34).

3. I am not sure what you have in mind in this part of your letter, especially in the concluding sentence: 'How would you advise me to deal with this particular thing', etc.

Now with warmest regards and appreciation,

Cordially Yours,
John Murray

P.S. My wife gave birth to a son on Dec. 22. Both are well and home with me since 30 Dec. JM.

Christ's Human Nature

Badbea
22 Nov. 1969

Dear Mr Green,

Thank you for your kind letter just received. I have no appointments in England until the Leicester Conference, 16–19 March. My wife and I are planning to go to the USA for two months at the end of December. We are all well. A journey so long with Logan young is an undertaking but we hope for the Lord's care and blessing.

The Reformed Churches in the Netherlands have now joined the World Council of Churches, another indication of the defection. The Church to which I belong in the States at its last meeting of the Assembly terminated sisterly relations with this denomination. That was a necessary breach.

In respect of his human nature our Lord's knowledge was *necessarily* limited. It was not a case of self-limitation except that in becoming human he did subject himself to all the sinless limitations and infirmities belonging to human nature. The same applies to ubiquity. Though omnipresent in respect of his deity, yet in his human nature he is not omnipresent. If he were he would cease to be human.

At the same time it is necessary to say, that it was *he*, the Son of God and by incarnation God-man, who was limited in these respects but limited in human nature, not in respect of deity.

As Messiah these were also self-accepted limitations arising from and belonging to the task he came to perform. These could be spoken of as self-limitations or self-restrictions (cf. e.g. *Matt.* 26:53).

With warmest regards and appreciation, dear friend,

I am,
Cordially Yours,
John Murray

P.S. Convey my kind regards to Mr Macmillan when you write him. JM.

CHRIST'S SONSHIP; REVELATION 20

Badbea
25 Nov. 1970

My Dear and Prized Friend,
Thanks for your letter just received. This reply will be little more than one of thanks and deep appreciation. I have so much on

hand that the lengthy reply your letter deserves is beyond me at present.

Yes, the Banner of Truth Trust has close links with Calvinists in the USA, especially with those associated with the witness in Carlisle, PA.

Respecting Christ's Sonship, I don't think we can attach more meaning to 'eternal generation' than that his Sonship is *eternal* and not derived from the economical undertakings and offices.

I totally reject the notion that the Son derives his deity from the Father. As to deity he is self-existent (αὐτόθεος) but his hypostatic differentiation is that he is *Son of the Father*. We cannot say much more. But there is much that is involved in the Sonship on which there is copious witness in the New Testament. As respects *Mark* 13:32 and parallels, we have to think of that which did not come within his human cognition but also as that which did not belong at that time to his messianic consciousness. There was conveyance to him in his messianic identity and offices. This detail in respect of day and hour had not been conveyed to him.

Respecting *Rev.* 20 we must keep in view the canons of interpretation that apply to the *visions* of the book as a whole. What is represented by the visions is not a literal fulfilment of the details but something far transcending. This principle has to be applied to *Rev.* 20. Now what in reality is represented is something on which I could not dare to be dogmatic. But an interpretation consonant with the terms necessary in other visions is reasonable and consistent with the analogy of Scripture, an interpretation that eliminates the notion of *a thousand year* reign in the chronology of world history.

With my warmest regards,
John Murray

Badbea,
19 July 1971

My Dear Friend,

I just received your second letter with enclosures. No, No, I have not been offended by anything you have written in your earlier letter. The *only* reason for my failure to reply is the difficulty under which I am labouring. Your questions would require a lengthy letter. I find it very arduous to write long letters. It would probably take me a whole day to answer your queries. But the real explanation is the fact that my wife is approaching another confinement and this with the care of an active 2½ year old boy involves me so much extra family responsibility and with that distraction that I am scarcely able to concentrate on what your questions demand. Please understand and remember that the years have taken their toll of my abilities.

I am,
Cordially Yours,
John Murray

Lloyd-Jones on Romans; Women in the Church

Badbea,
30 Jan. 1974

My Dear Friend,

I am delighted to have your letter of the 25th. It came yesterday but I was prostrate with gastric flu and my wife brought me no mail; she thought I was too sick.

I have all of Dr Lloyd-Jones' books on Romans hitherto published. I am pleased to know they have been so helpful to you. They are distinctly practical. I cannot make much of his exposition of *Rom.* 7:14–25: he seems to vacillate so much. But there are still a few pages I have to read.

The Banner of Truth plans to publish a book of mine soon comprising some new material but mostly articles published years ago in Journals, etc.

I think the exegesis of *1 Tim.* 2:8–9 to which you refer is exegetically monstrous. It is obvious that the ὡσαύτως (vs. 9) harks back to Βούλομαι (vs. 8) and that the verb going with the same in vs. 9 is κοσμεῖν parallel to προσεύχεσθαι in vs. 8. The absurdity of the exegesis you refer to appears when we ask the question: how is the structure of vs. 9 to be conceived if 'likewise also the women' is to be covered by προσεύχεσθαι?

I am thankful to say we are all well. The children are growing fast: Logan is 5, Anne-Margaret 2½. I am preaching regularly. But, in view of the senility of my sister, now 88, I am not able to go far from home. Scarcely ever am I able to be away overnight. So I don't get to Leicester any more.

Our national situation is desperate. I fear your assessment is correct.

Now with my warmest personal regards and thanks for your letter,

I am,
Affectionately Yours,
John Murray

THE TWO NATURES OF CHRIST

Badbea,
22 Nov. 1974

My Dear Friend,

It is a pleasure to hear from you. How good it would be if only we could meet face to face and discuss the questions you raise – 'iron sharpeneth iron, so the countenance of a man his friend'.

With respect to 1. I need not say anything. Your reflections are correct.

2. We must hold to a twofold consciousness but at the same time to one self-consciousness. There is evidence from the Gospels that even when our Lord was acting and speaking in terms of the limitations belonging to his human nature and imposed upon him in terms of his commission, he did not identify himself in terms of human personality but in terms of his divine person. I cannot now adduce the relevant instances. But *Mark* 13:32 illustrates. He identifies himself as the Son – 'neither the Son, but the Father only'. The title as well as the contrast with the Father point to the intradivine Sonship, and so in that notable instance of limitation it is as divine 'self' he speaks and as divine 'self' predicates of himself the not-knowing involved. Hence I think Chalcedon showed most commendable insight on the question at stake.

3. We may never entertain the thought of an abridged deity and therefore not of an abridged divine consciousness. How omniscience could coexist with the limited knowledge of his human cognition is just another aspect, perhaps accentuates for our understanding, of the ineffable system of two distinct natures in one person, two distinct sets of attributes diverse from each other in respect of quality and scope.

4. This is a difficult question. I think it is related to what I was dealing with last Sabbath night on *Eph.* 1:23 – 'filleth all in all'. This may not be your precise problem. But may I reproduce my thoughts on this expression? It refers to that which is applied to Christ as the God-man and head over all things to his body, the church. I take it in conjunction with *Eph.* 4:10 – 'that he might fill all things' – and refers to what *occurred* in the ascension. How could Jesus *come* to fill all things when as respects his deity he already filled all things by omnipresence? My exposition was to this effect. Although Jesus' human nature never did or could become omnipresent and

although as respects deity he was always omnipresent as Creator and upholder of all, yet by the ascension to the right hand of power a new relation to the universe was constituted and therefore a new relation for his omnipresence in respect of his deity. Now as the *God-man* and *head over all things to the church* he fills all things (filleth all in all). This could only be in respect of his deity (manhood could not fill all things) but his deity in his identity as God-man and head over all to the church, an identity that was not his essentially but only by incarnation and the sequels culminating in the ascension. This is an exceedingly precious ingredient of faith, to know that all the attributes and prerogatives of deity are brought to bear upon the exercise of his investiture as head over all on behalf of the church.

Of course the expressions in Ephesians bear also upon the universal dominion he has come to exercise as God-man.

We are all well. Logan is nearing six and is now in school. Anne-Margaret is three and four months. How thankful we should be for numberless blessings!

With warm affection,
I am,
Most Cordially,
John Murray

P.S. Please understand that because of various pressures, family, preaching, correspondence etc. I am not able to devote as much time to your deeply appreciated letter as I would like. JM.